Ewan McGregor

AN ILLUSTRATED STORY

DAVID BASSOM

HAMLYN

Acknowledgments
The author would like to thank Jedi Master
Julian Brown, Emperor Tarda Davison-
Aitkins, Princess Karen O'Grady and all at
Hamlyn for their continued support,
encouragement and employment. Kudos
also to Robert Hull, Marcus Hearn, Anwar
Brett, Jerry Cheung, David Miller and
Anthony Lavelle for various pointers along
the way, and to Mum, Dad and Danny for
being such an inspiration over the years.
May the Force be with you all ...

Publishing Director: Laura Bamford
Executive Editor: Julian Brown
Editor: Tarda Davison-Aitkins
Executive Art Editor: Mark Stevens
Design: Steve Byrne
Picture Research: Liz Fowler
Production: Clare Smedley

Picture Acknowledgements

The Publisher wishes to thank the following
organizations for their kind permission to
reproduce the photographs in this book:

All Action /Pat/Arnal/Geral 40 centre
Alpha 26-27, 54-55, 56 top, 57, 78 bottom;
/Randolph Caughie 8-9, 10 bottom, 40 bottom;
/Richard Chambury 66
British Film Institute Stills, Posters & Designs 10
top
Camera Press 18-19, 21; /Mark Shenley 76; /John
Timbers 22 top, 23; /TSPL 11, 15; /Oliver Upton 20;
/Theodore Wood 42, 64
Colorific Photo Library /Theo Kingma 62
Corbis UK Ltd/Everett 24-25, 26, 28-29, 32-33, 33
top, 48 bottom, 52, 55, 58 top, 79;
/Darren Michaels 49; /David Appleby 46-47; /Robert
Zuckerman 50-51
Famous /Paul Brookes 43 bottom
Kobal Collection /Film Four/Pandora/Skreba/Liam
Longman 31 top; /Kasander &Wigman/Alpha
Films/Marc Guillamot 33 bottom; /Lucasfilm/20th
Century Fox 12 bottom, 62-63, 68
Pictorial Press/PolyGram 34-35, 36-37, 38, 39
centre, 40 top, 40-41, 78 left; /Liam Daniel 39 top,
39 bottom
Retna /Jim Cooper 69; /Armando Gallo 76-77;
/Steve Granitz 56 bottom; /Keibun Miyamoto 18, 59
70/Valletoux/Studio/MPA 8; /Theodore Wood 31
bottom
Rex Features 16-17, 51 top, 58 bottom, 60-61;
/Dobson Agency 72, 74, 75; /Heptagon 43 top;
/J. Sutton Hibbert 6-7, 12-13, 14; /Steve Hill 22
bottom; /David Sandison 2-3, 5, 80; /SIPA Press 72-
73
The Ronald Grant Archive 30, 44, 51 bottom, 78
top; /Film Four Distributors/ David Appleby 48 top;
/Lucasfilm/20th Century Fox 12 top, 65

First published in Great Britain in 1998
by Hamlyn, an imprint of
Octopus Publishing Group Limited
Michelin House, 81 Fulham Road, London SW3 6RB

Copyright © 1998 Octopus Publishing Group Limited

ISBN 0 600 59653 2

A catalogue record for this book is available from the British Library

Printed in the United States of America

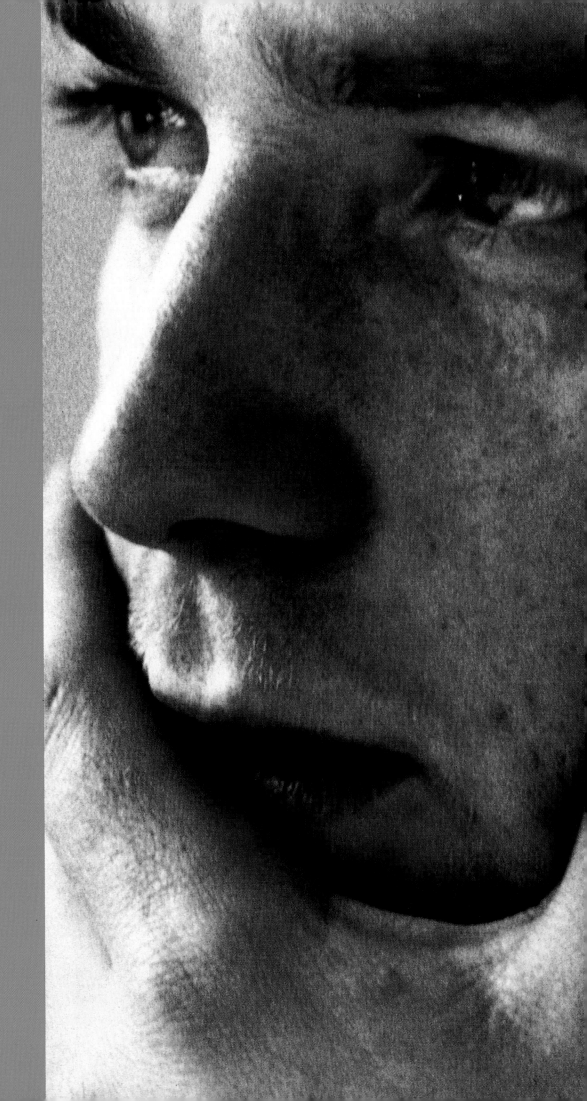

Contents

REBEL WITH A CAUSE

From high school drop-out to international star and cultural icon, Ewan McGregor has become one of the world's hottest actors

As a child growing up in the conservative community of Crieff, Scotland, Ewan McGregor soon began to dream of a life less ordinary and looked to the arts – especially music and acting – as a means of escapism

He's been hailed as one of the finest actor of his generation, Britain's coolest leading man since Michael Caine and Scotland's most popular export since Sean Connery. He's successfully dodged the potential pitfalls and perils of overnight fame playing a diverse range of roles in an eclectic series of film and television productions. And thanks to the eagerly-awaited new Star Wars films, he's set to become one of the most well-known and beloved actors in the galaxy. Meet Ewan McGregor: a 1990s' acting sensation whose star is destined to shine well into the new millennium.

In little more than a decade, Ewan McGregor has transformed himself from high school drop-out to international celebrity and cultural icon. After leaving school at 16 without any qualifications, the aspiring actor was plucked from the obscurity of drama school to star in his first TV series, *Lipstick on Your Collar*. A steady stream of projects followed, culminating in breakthrough performances in *Shallow Grave* and the unforgettable *Trainspotting*. The critical and commercial success of both films swiftly established McGregor as one of the hottest young talents around, and earned him further roles in projects ranging from the contemporary dramas *Brassed Off* and *Rogue Trader* to the whimsical love story *A Life Less Ordinary* and the outrageous Glam Rock opera *Velvet Goldmine*, to name but a few.

Rebel with a Cause

Above: **Although McGregor had a difficult time at school, he was given a hero's welcome when he returned to Morrison's Academy post-*Trainspotting* to give an acting seminar**

Top: **Denis Lawson's unconventional lifestyle caught the imagination of his nephew, who began to view the actor as a role model**

However, the diversity of McGregor's work and his ability to consistently generate that oft-elusive blend of critical acclaim and mass appeal are just two of the elements which have made the young Scottish actor stand apart from many of his contemporaries. A third distinguishing feature concerns his impact on popular culture. As the star of *Trainspotting*, McGregor offered an uncompromising portrait of alienated youth which struck a chord with teenage and twentysomething cinemagoers around the world. Since then, he has remained on the cutting-edge of the *Zeitgeist*, where he is fast becoming 'Cooldom' personified. This trend was set to continue with the release of the new *Star Wars* movies, guaranteeing Ewan a place in the hearts and minds of viewers of all ages.

Perhaps most impressive of all, though, McGregor is one of those rare talents who has managed to rise to the upper echelons of the entertainment industry without bowing to its conventions.

After rocketing to fame in the title role of *Trainspotting*, the daring Scot rejected the inevitable call of Hollywood and all its lucrative trappings, choosing instead to remain in Britain, where he continued to pursue a career driven by artistic merit rather than commerce. He has also maintained his commitment to the cause of challenging film-making, playing the likes of drug addicts, bisexual rock stars and convicted criminals in a candid and unadulterated manner, which would have most established leading men running for cover.

McGregor is as much the maverick behind the camera. He remains blissfully unaffected by the hype surrounding his extraordinary career and utterly refuses to play the 'Fame Game', shunning showbiz schmoozing in favour of spending time with old friends or playing the devoted family man with his wife and daughter. Consequently, McGregor is still every inch the 'Boy Next Door' – albeit one who has been embraced by neighbours of all race, colour and gender across the globe!

The full story of Ewan McGregor's meteoric rise is a potent Scottish brew, the key ingredients being talent, enthusiasm, hard work and a willingness to take risks – all mixed together with that extra special Force known as luck.

It begins in Crieff, a small town on the edge of the Scottish Highlands, which was previously synonymous with the actor's namesake, Rob Roy MacGregor. In the 18th century, Crieff had been the site of some of Rob Roy's bloodiest struggles against his English enemies. 300 years later, it would play host to another McGregor whose exploits were set to become the stuff of legend.

Born on 31st March 1971 at the Perth Royal Infirmary, Ewan Gordon McGregor was the second son of James and Carol McGregor, arriving a little over two years after the birth of his elder brother, Colin. Together, both children were destined to have a happy and extremely stable upbringing in Crieff, a sleepy, conservative, middle-class town which was most notable for its extremely low crime rate and was fast becoming one of Scotland's leading retirement resorts.

Ewan's education began in a private nursery in Crieff Hydro, and at the age of five he joined the primary section of Morrison's Academy, a highly-respected institution where his father, James, had once studied and now taught. Although Morrison's was a boarding school, the two McGregor boys attended as day students. By all accounts, young Ewan was a quiet and well-behaved pupil, with a gift for charming teachers and classmates alike.

From an early age, the future star demonstrated a healthy interest in the Arts, and was said to be extremely creative. His musical talents in particular seemed to know no bounds. At home, he would dazzle family and friends with his Elvis Presley impressions, while in the classroom, McGregor was renowned for his versatility. He played the drums with both the school pipe band and a local ceilidh group, won a school prize for his accomplished use of the French horn, sang with the school choir, and was a keen guitarist. During the latter part of his school years, McGregor also served as the drummer with a local rock band, Scarlet Pride – a task which required him to douse his hair with red paint and wear bandanas around his knees. McGregor even excelled at Scottish country dancing, much to the amusement of most of his friends!

Although music was McGregor's first love and his original childhood dream was to

be a rock star, by the age of nine he had abandoned that idea in favour of a career as an actor. McGregor always loved old black and white movies and would give children's TV programmes a miss in favour of the Ealing comedies and Hollywood romances from the 1940s and 1950s. He also enjoyed going to pantomimes, where he particularly savoured the sight of actresses' legs in fishnet stockings!

Probably the biggest impulse for McGregor's change of career plans, though, came from his uncle, actor Denis Lawson. After studying drama in Glasgow, Lawson had moved to London in the early 1970s to launch a steady career which would encompass the likes of *Providence*, *The Chain* and the immensely popular Bill Forsyth film *Local Hero*. His unconventional lifestyle and celebrity status were always admired by his nephew, who was fast becoming tired with life in staid Crieff. And

as time went on, he began to view Lawson as a role model.

'I looked up to him because he was different,' McGregor later explained to *Ministry* magazine. 'Growing up in the 1970s, I came from this small, conservative place and he used to come up from London in sheepskin waistcoats, beads, long hair, no shoes, and he'd give you flowers and stuff. I thought, "Who is this man? He's incredible!" At that point, he was so different – and I felt the need to be different too.'

Lawson rose further in McGregor's estimation by starring in three of his all-time favourite films: *Star Wars*, *The Empire Strikes Back* and *Return of the Jedi*. As the heroic X-Wing pilot Wedge Antilles, Uncle Denis was instrumental in the destruction of two Death Stars and the ultimate downfall of the evil Empire – and even lived to tell the tale!

McGregor saw *Star Wars* for the first time at the beginning of 1978, at Perth's Odeon

Inspired by a genuine love of films, the example of his uncle Denis and his own experiences on stage, McGregor had set his heart on becoming an actor by the age of nine

Rebel with a Cause

Like most young boys at the time, McGregor was awe-struck by seeing *Star Wars* for the first time – and also developed a crush on the film's leading lady, Carrie Fisher

Cinema. Like most viewers his age, the six-year-old was simply mesmerised by George Lucas's ground-breaking science-fiction adventure movie. Within days of seeing the film, young McGregor's room was packed with various pieces of *Star Wars* merchandise including sheets and pillow cases, while at school he would join in with playground re-enactments of scenes from the movie. He also developed a crush on the film's leading lady, Carrie Fisher, who would only be replaced as the object of his affections many months later, by Olivia Newton-John when he saw the smash hit musical *Grease*.

Driven by a genuine passion for films and inspired by his uncle's example, McGregor increasingly felt drawn to the thought of acting for a living and had set his heart on the idea by his ninth birthday. By then, he had already gained some experience of the profession – albeit at an amateur level.

During the summer of 1977, five-year-old Ewan McGregor made his acting debut as the villainous Sheriff of Nottingham in a school production of *Robin Hood*. He then took the lead role in an adaptation of *David and Goliath* the following year. Even at this early age, McGregor showed both a flair for acting and a commitment to his work. Not only were his teachers surprised by the quality of his performance, but they were particularly impressed that he had managed to learn and remember all his lines at a time when he was still mastering the art of reading!

Unfortunately, however, while McGregor was showing great promise as an actor and musician, his performance in the classroom was less impressive. By the time he had entered the secondary wing of Morrison's Academy, it was clear that his heart really wasn't in his school work and he was struggling to keep up to standard with the traditionally-important subjects, namely English, Maths and Science. He was even having difficulty with Physical Education (P.E.) lessons, much to the discomfort of his teacher/father, James McGregor. These problems were only ex-acerbated by the fact that his brother, Colin, had emerged as an A-grade student who seemed to excel at every subject, including P.E., and had been appointed as the school's Head Boy.

Ewan's situation only worsened over time. At 15, he was told that he had to drop either

Art or Music, in favour of a more academic subject. He had also started to feel that he didn't fit in, as his hopes and dreams seemed a world apart from those of his classmates. Faced with such difficulties, McGregor's behaviour predictably began to deteriorate, and the young student was frequently sent to see the school's Deputy Headmaster.

'I wasn't much interested in school,' McGregor subsequently admitted in an interview in *Film Review*. 'I got into trouble all the time and they kept saying, "Attitude Problem!" I was unaware I had one *because*

I had one, and it was starting to embarrass my father.'

Entering his fifth year at senior school, McGregor's prospects of passing his all-important Higher National exams looked grim. He had barely scraped through his mocks, with the exception of Maths, which he subsequently dropped in favour of a typing course. With the pressure mounting and his interest continuing to wane, McGregor realised that he 'just couldn't hack it any more'. Fortunately, his caring parents had reached the same conclusion and decided to

make their son an offer which would change his life forever.

'I was driving into Crieff with my mum and it was pouring with rain,' he recalled in *Ministry*. 'I remember the windscreen wipers were smacking about and she turned to me and said, "Listen, I've spoken to your father and if you want to leave school, then you can, if you like." I was 16. I'd just imagined I'd have to go through two more years of school. I never imagined that I could leave and I said, "Right, I'll leave".'

News of McGregor's early exit from school stunned the people of Crieff, who could not

With his parents' blessing, McGregor left school at the age of 16 without any qualifications to pursue a professional career as an actor. After gaining work experience at Perth Repertory Theatre, he landed a place to study drama at Kirkcaldy College of Technology

While attending the Guildhall School of Music and Drama, McGregor was trained in virtually every aspect of the acting profession, from auditioning for roles right through to publicising projects. Sadly, however, there was nothing on the course to prepare him for the adoring crowds or the process of signing hundreds of autographs at a time!

understand such unconformist behaviour. However, his parents had decided that they simply could not prolong his suffering any further and gave him their total support as he launched himself into the 'Real World'.

With the help of his mother, McGregor quickly landed his first full-time job as a £50-a-week stagehand at Perth Repertory Theatre. Perth had produced a number of successful actors, including Gordon Jackson (of *Upstairs Downstairs* and *The Professionals* fame) and Edward Woodward (*Callan*, *The Equalizer*), so it promised to give McGregor a good grounding in the profession.

At Perth, McGregor immediately stood out for his enthusiasm, willingness to learn, devotion to duty – and his blond spiky haircut, which he modelled after his rock idol of the time, Billy Idol. The young actor gained invaluable experience in all aspects of the acting profession, from moving stage scenery to working in front of a paying audience. His first professional appearance came in the theatre's production of *A Passage to India*, in which he donned a turban to play an extra.

McGregor's sixth months at Perth also played a crucial role in landing him a place to study drama at Kirkcaldy College of Technology. After attending an audition and an interview, the aspiring actor became one of just 26 students who were offered a place on the course. In August 1988, McGregor loaded his Volkswagen Beetle and left Crieff for his new home on the college campus in Fife.

During his nine months at Kirkcaldy, McGregor had to study virtually every aspect of acting, from performance and dance right through to stage-construction and publicity. He starred in a series of college productions, including *The Prime of Miss Jean Brodie*, *A Few from the Fridge* and *Missfoot*, while his end of year tests included a soliloquy from Shakespeare's *Twelfth Night* and a spoof of the 1960s' TV series *Batman*. According to his classmates, McGregor's unique talent was clear even at this early stage.

It was at Kirkcaldy that McGregor first began to realise how relatively easy and painless his upbringing had been. When he and his classmates were asked to discuss their life stories and share some of their most painful experiences, the young Scot found that he simply couldn't compete with the tales of angst and despair offered by those around him.

McGregor's natural charm with the female of the species also came to the fore at college. He had always been popular with girls from an early age, enjoying his first kiss at nine years old. At Kirkcaldy, however, he dated no less than four of the girls on his course, including Hannah Titley, with whom he forged his first serious relationship.

Upon completing his course in the summer of 1989, McGregor left Kirkcaldy armed with a Higher National Certificate in Theatre Arts. He immediately took a job as a waiter in an Edinburgh pizza parlour, from where he planned his next move. After careful consideration, he decided that his future lay outside Scotland and decided to continue his education in London.

'In Scotland, there are people who want to stay there and do predominantly left-wing gay theatre,' Said McGregor later, telling *Elle* magazine about his decision to leave his homeland. 'If you're interested in it, that's what you'd probably be doing, which is good, but not necessarily for me all the time. I wanted to do whatever I chose.'

Much to his delight, McGregor was granted an interview for a place at the Royal Academy of Dramatic Arts (RADA), Britain's leading drama school. With the help of Uncle Denis, the young hopeful spent weeks preparing for the fateful meeting. Ultimately, though, it was not to be, as the future film and TV star was ignominiously rejected by the prestigious institution. McGregor was left devastated by the experience. Not only did it suggest that he wasn't equipped for the 'Big Time', but it also left him broke, as the interview cost him £30 (to cover RADA's administration fees) and a further £60 worth of travel expenses!

Fortunately, McGregor's talent was appreciated elsewhere. Shortly after the RADA rejection, he was offered an interview by the Guildhall School of Music and Drama,

and subsequently emerged as one of the 26 students chosen from 700 hopefuls to attend the three-year course.

Guildhall's driving goal was to prepare its students for professional acting careers, so its drama course was broadly broken up into three stages: the first year focused on acting theory; the second on actual performance; and the third at connecting students with agents and potential employers. Part of McGregor's training involved a tour of Europe, during which he played Orlando in a production of *As You Like It*.

Besides offering him a further chance to hone his craft, McGregor's three years at Guildhall also enabled him to grow accustomed to living in London. The young Scot swiftly fell in love with the capital's cosmopolitan atmosphere as well as the wide range of acting roles that were on offer, and would make London his home long after he had completed his education.

Ultimately, however, Ewan McGregor's time at Guildhall would provide him with more than just a dress rehearsal for his future career. As the end of his studies drew near, the aspiring actor would find himself presented with his first big break, taking a leading role in a major television production.

Lady thriller: McGregor was always popular with the ladies, enjoying his first kiss at the age of nine and dating a string of girls while at school and college. Stardom would only increase this trend by making him an international pin-up and heart-throb

2

Before he had even completed his acting course, McGregor was cast in his first major TV role

Above: McGregor thought that disaster had struck when he forgot his lines during his Guildhall showcase, but his performance was still good enough to land him an audition for a leading role in the TV mini-series *Lipstick on your Collar*

Opposite: To play Private Mick Hopper, a jaded translator who dreams of becoming a rock 'n' roll star, McGregor was not only required to act, sing, dance and lip sync, but also had to adopt an English accent and dye his hair black

At the beginning of 1992, the third-year students of the Guildhall School of Music and Drama prepared for their final year showcase. The event offered thema unique opportunity to demonstrate their potential in front of some 200 casting agents and directors, and could therefore be a passport to instant fame and fortune.

Among these hopefuls was Ewan McGregor, whose eclectic presentation consisted of a Barbra Streisand song, an extract from the cult movie *Withnail & I*, an original monologue about a crippled oil rig worker which the actor had written himself, and a cover version of the Bill Withers soul classic *Lean on Me*. Unfortunately, it was not McGregor's lucky night. For although his showcase opened extremely well, tragedy struck just over the halfway mark, when he momentarily forgot his lines while performing his monologue. With that brief lapse of concentration, McGregor's chances of winning a patron from his audience went up in smoke.

Or so it seemed. In reality, however, McGregor's work had managed to catch the imagination of one agent, Lindy King. King was involved with the casting of a new TV mini-series for Channel 4 called *Lipstick on your Collar*, and had spent several months looking for a young leading man who could

Swing Shift

Lipstick on your Collar **allowed McGregor to demonstrate his full potential as a multi-talented performer, in a production which veered between hard-hitting drama scenes and surreal musical numbers**

not only act, but could also sing, dance and lip-sync accurately. After seeing the all-singing, all-acting McGregor in action, King began to wonder if she had finally found him and expressed an interest in representing McGregor. It was an offer he simply could not refuse.

Immediately after the showcase, King arranged a meeting between McGregor and the show's producer, Rosemarie Whitman, and its choreographer, Quinny Sacks. After a brief discussion about the project, McGregor was invited to audition for the part by miming to the classic Elvis Presley track, *Hound Dog*. The actor immediately unveiled the Elvis impersonation he had originally perfected as a child and completely bowled-over his two-strong audience. By the next day, the role was his for the taking.

Once again, Ewan McGregor had defied the odds. Before he had even finished studying at Guildhall, he had been plucked from total obscurity to play a leading role in a major television production. *Lipstick on your*

Collar was the latest offering from Dennis Potter, the controversial playwright whose prolific output included *Pennies from Heaven*, *Brimstone and Treacle*, *Blackeyes* and the award-winning *Singing Detective.* As such, it was one of Channel 4's most high-profile and ambitious projects of the year.

Filming was scheduled to start in March, and lasted seven months. McGregor originally planned to combine shooting with the remainder of his studies at Guildhall, but after much thought, concluded that his role in *Lipstick on your Collar* was simply too demanding and time-consuming to be combined with college commitments. Consequently, some three months before graduation, the high school drop-out reluctantly decided to leave acting school. It was a difficult choice, but one that he would never regret.

Upon reporting to the show's production base at Twickenham Studios in London, McGregor was introduced to his three co-stars, Giles Thomas, Louise Germaine and Kimberley Huffman. Like the young Scot, they were all unknown and relatively in-experienced and viewed *Lipstick on your Collar* as their ticket to the Big Time. Clearly, Potter's latest brainchild was not going to be a conventional production.

Set in the 1950s, the six-part mini-series follows the exploits of a Welsh military intelligence officer, Private Francis Francis (Thomas) and his best friend, jaded translator Private Mick Hopper (McGregor, sporting jet-black hair and an English accent). As the end of their army service draws near, Hopper dreams of pursuing a new career as a drummer and, in a series of surreal musical sequences, imagines himself performing various rock 'n' roll hits while his colleagues provide backing vocals.

Lipstick on your Collar represented a brilliant start to McGregor's professional acting career. Not only was he starring in a major television production, but his role as Hopper allowed him to demonstrate his full range as a multi-talented performer and, in a sense, fulfil his childhood dream of singing and dancing for a living. It was an opportunity the young unknown relished, and he was destined to be remembered as one of the show's strongest elements.

McGregor also seized the chance to learn everything he possibly could about the demands and practicalities of television production. Like at Perth Repertory Theatre, he would be remembered by his colleagues for his enthusiasm, willingness to learn and commitment to work, all of which made him one of the most popular members of the production.

One of the actor's new-found friends included Dennis Potter, who spent a great deal of time with McGregor discussing a wide range of subjects, including the demands and dangers of fame. McGregor developed a deep respect for the renowned writer and would heed his warning. Potter also joined McGregor and his parents for dinner one evening, when he complemented their son's work. This was music to James and Carol's ears, as it suggested that their faith in Ewan wasn't misplaced. Touched by Potter's kindness, McGregor would return the favour some four years later, by making a brief cameo appearance in the playwright's final work, *Karaoke*.

Although *Lipstick on your Collar* ceased production at the end of August 1992, the series would not receive its premiere until February the following year. McGregor spent the best part of six months waiting with bated breath for the transmission of his first TV production, which he hoped would establish him as an exciting new talent and thus lead to a series of challenging screen roles.

Ultimately, however, he would be disappointed. When *Lipstick on your Collar* finally did reach the small screen, it was given a thumbs-down by most critics (who labelled it as one of Potter's less-memorable works), while the majority of viewers simply gave it a miss. McGregor nevertheless, won some excellent notices for his outstanding screen debut. Naturally, the show's lacklustre reception was a huge blow for its young star and an event from which he would learn an important lesson.

'I thought when *Lipstick* was aired, my life would change dramatically,' he later admitted. 'I counted the days to the first transmission. But nothing happened. Nobody recognised me – I didn't get mobbed. It was a huge anti-climax. Since then I've learned that nothing changes.'

To make matters even worse, during the interim period between the production and transmission of *Lipstick on your Collar*, McGregor had found work hard to come by. With only an unseen TV series to his credit, the inexperienced and unknown actor faced rejection after rejection. After a while, he even began to think that he wouldn't work again.

Fortunately, McGregor's run of bad luck came to an end when he landed a minor role in *Being Human*, an offbeat film drama starring Hollywood superstar Robin Williams and directed by Scottish film-maker Bill Forsyth (*Gregory's Girl*, *Local Hero*). The movie follows Williams through five lives – those of a caveman, Roman slave, Irishman,

Despite an unforgettable turn from McGregor, *Lipstick on your Collar* proved to be a critical and commercial disappointment, which left the young actor desperately seeking further work

Above: **McGregor was delighted to land the leading role in the prestigious BBC mini-series *Scarlet and Black*, and thoroughly enjoyed the seven-week shoot - including the numerous nudes scenes!**

Opposite page: **Many critics claimed that McGregor was simply too young and handsome to play the scheming Julien Sorel, but female viewers had no such complaints!**

shipwrecked traveller and contemporary American respectively – and attempts to explore the primary driving forces of life. McGregor makes his brief feature film debut as a shipwrecked Portuguese sailor who has precisely two lines of dialogue.

While it was hardly challenging or rewarding work, *Being Human* did provide McGregor with a free trip to North Africa and a chance to study the process of big-budget film-making. It also enabled him to see a major Hollywood star in action. Sadly, though, the film would do little for McGregor's career, especially after it bombed at the American box office.

Returning to British shores, McGregor spent the early part of 1993 appearing in a stage production of the Joe Orton play, *What the Butler Saw*, at Salisbury Playhouse. As Nick, the actor's most notable contribution to proceedings was streaking across the stage – twice! This would certainly not be the last time that McGregor was required to appear nude for his art.

McGregor's next performance came in *Family Style*, an 11-minute black and white short directed by his friend, Justin Chadwick, and produced for Channel 4 as part of the Lloyd's Bank Young Writers' Challenge. This little-seen film stars McGregor as a Yorkshire teenager who struggles to come to terms with a bereavement.

Family Style offered a complete contrast to McGregor's next project, *Scarlet and Black*. A lavish BBC costume drama based on Stendhal's classic French novel, *Le Rouge et le Noir*, *Scarlet and Black* follows the adventures of Julien Sorel, a swashbuckling young hero who rises from peasantry to the highest tiers of Parisian society, before his untimely demise.

The series required a strong and handsome leading man, who was equally adept at love scenes as he was at epic fight sequences. A host of actors read for the role, including McGregor, who attended his first audition just before Christmas 1992. Although he left the meeting convinced that he had blown his chances, producer Ros Wolfes and director Ben Bolt were impressed by his efforts. After gaining an exclusive sneak preview of his work in *Lipstick on your Collar*, the pair realised that they had found their

leading man. McGregor was promptly called in for a second meeting, which he left with the knowledge that the role was his.

Filmed in Britain and France and earmarked for a prime-time slot, *Scarlet and Black* was a prestigious production indeed. As with *Lipstick on your Collar*, McGregor rose to the challenge and worked hard throughout the seven-week shoot. He relished the chance to shoot fight scenes and horse riding sequences, doing many of his own his stunts.

The project also required McGregor to film a string of passionate love scenes with his two co-stars, Alice Krige (*Chariots of Fire*, *Star Trek: First Contact*) and Rachel Weisz (*Chain Reaction*), and to bare all in a few sequences. For one such shot, McGregor had to run through a French field completely nude – an experience he later described as being 'nice'! Clearly, the actor had no problem with going *au natural* in front of the camera, and it would swiftly become one of the many trademarks of his work.

'I've been naked in almost everything I've been in really,' he later joked in *Elle*. 'In fact, I have it written into my contract!'

Scarlet and Black received its British television premiere during the autumn of 1993, when it won mixed reviews at best. Most critics accused the adaptation of being unfaithful to Stendhal's novel, and particularly objected to McGregor's casting in the lead role, on the grounds that he was simply too young and handsome to play Julien Sorel.

Such views weren't shared by the viewing public, however, who made the three-part series a huge success, with an average audience of over 10 million viewers. McGregor's leading performance instantly established him as one of British TV's hottest new properties and he soon found himself inundated with fan mail for first time in his career. Impressively, most viewers were fooled by his English accent, and didn't suspect for one second that their new heart-throb was a Scotsman!

Coupled with his work in *Lipstick on your Collar*, *Scarlet and Black* proved that Ewan McGregor could command viewers' attention with breathtaking ease. He would demonstrate this skill on the big screen with his next project, *Shallow Grave*.

DEEP IMPACT

3

Shallow Grave firmly placed McGregor at the cutting edge of British cinema, and underlined his star potential

Produced on a shoestring budget by relatively unknown film-makers, *Shallow Grave* marked Ewan McGregor's first step towards big-screen fame and fortune

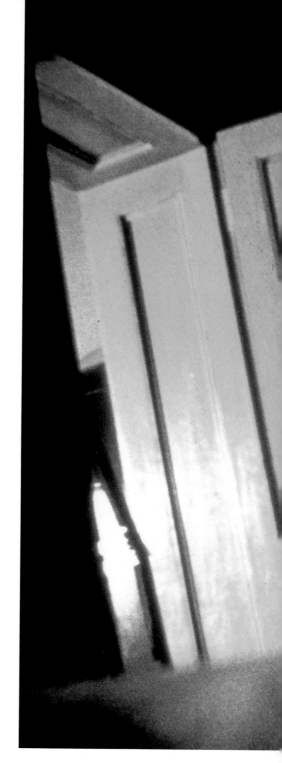

Shortly after *Scarlet and Black* ceased filming, producer Ros Wolfes received a telephone call from an up-and-coming director named Danny Boyle. The pair had previously collaborated together on another BBC production, *Mr Wroe's Virgins*, and Boyle was now in the process of casting his first feature film. The movie was called *Shallow Grave* and required a young Scottish actor as one of its three leads. Boyle had heard about Wolfes's new discovery, Ewan McGregor, and was calling to ask if she could recommend him for the part. Her reply was destined to take the actor's career to new heights and would mark the beginning of a celebrated partnership.

A tale of three flatmates who become embroiled in a web of murder, deceit and betrayal, *Shallow Grave* began life in 1991 as the brainchild of junior doctor and would-be screenwriter John Hodge. While attending the Edinburgh International Film Festival that year, Hodge pitched his idea to an aspiring producer called Andrew Macdonald. Macdonald had worked in various capacities on a number of projects, including *Revolution*, *Venus Peter* and the TV drama *Taggart*, and was also the grandson of Emeric Pressburger who, together with Michael Powell, had directed such cinematic classics as *A Matter of Life and Death*, *Black Narcissus* and *The*

Red Shoes. He instantly liked Hodge's idea and the pair soon turned their attention to getting the project off the ground.

Their first breakthrough came in July 1992, when the Scottish Film Production Fund provided the team with £4,000 to develop Hodge's script – a figure which was doubled to allow them to complete the task. After a grand total of 12 rewrites, Hodge's script was finally optioned in January 1993 by Channel 4 who, together with the Glasgow Film Production Unit, would supply *Shallow Grave*'s budget of just over £1 million.

With funding secured, Macdonald and Hodge's next task was to choose a director. Both agreed that they wanted someone who shared their vision of the project, and who also saw film-making as a collaborative process. After much deliberation, the job went to Danny Boyle, whose credits included the BBC TV mini-series *Mr Wroe's Virgins* and two episodes of the popular ITV drama *Inspector Morse*.

Boyle immediately turned his attention to the casting of *Shallow Grave*'s three leading characters, a process which he knew would be crucial to the film's success. With Macdonald and Hodge's blessing, the first person he hired was Kerry Fox, a New Zealand-born actress who had won widespread acclaim for her work in *An Angel At My Table* and came fresh from starring in Boyle's last project, *Mr Wroe's Virgins*. The next actor cast was Christopher Eccleston, following his impressive performances in the film drama *Let Him Have It* and the TV series *Cracker*. The third and final role would go to Ewan McGregor, who was recommended for the part by Ros Wolfes having fought off strong

On discovering a dead flatmate and a suitcase full of money, Juliet (Kerry Fox), Alex (McGregor) and David (Christopher Eccleston) decide to keep the cash for themselves and bury the evidence in a shallow grave

To create a sense of familiarity between Fox, Eccleston and McGregor which befitted long-time flatmates, the three actors actually shared a flat prior to the start of filming *Shallow Grave*

competition from the likes of rising star Robert Carlyle (*Priest*).

From the first time he saw the film's script, McGregor felt that *Shallow Grave* had the potential to be something special. An innovative blend of comedy, drama and horror, the film opens on a surprisingly innocuous note, with three flatmates, Juliet (Fox), David (Eccleston) and Alex (McGregor), advertising for a fourth lodger to share their home in Edinburgh's New Town. After a series of interviews with prospective lodgers, they rent the room to a mysterious novelist, Hugo (*The Comic Strip*'s Keith Allen).

Shortly after Hugo's arrival, however, his three flatmates find him dead from a drug overdose, lying next to a suitcase full of money. Fuelled by greed, Juliet, David and Alex decide to keep the cash for themselves and dispose of Hugo's body in a shallow grave. But the group's joy soon turns to despair when they come under scrutiny from both the local police and Hugo's former business associates.

Prior to the start of shooting, *Shallow Grave* required six weeks of pre-production, including a week of rehearsals in Glasgow, Scotland. At Boyle's behest, the cast and

and a door there; but we were in a real flat, so there was a wall there. It allowed us to get used to each other at the same time as getting used to our characters.'

On a more personal level, McGregor also prepared for his role as the acerbic journalist Alex Law by listening to tapes of various comedians, including Billy Connolly, Dennis Leary and The Jerky Boys, and by watching real-life journalists in action in the offices of *The Evening Times* newspaper in Glasgow. The actor later admitted that the biggest surprise about his research was just how much time journalists spend in front of a computer and on the phone.

From the outset, McGregor's main goal for *Shallow Grave* was to portray Alex as 'a loveable bastard.' While the character is undeniably rude, arrogant and greedy, his real-life alter ego tried to evoke some sympathy for him by emphasising such elements as Alex's desperate yearning for his flatmate, Juliet.

One thing McGregor didn't have to work at, though, was Alex Law's accent, which merely required him to employ his normal Scottish brogue. Ironically, however, McGregor had grown accustomed to

Despite its tight budget and breakneck shooting schedule, McGregor savoured his experience on *Shallow Grave*, and looked forward to working with director Danny Boyle, producer Andrew Macdonald and writer John Hodge again

crew actually shared a flat during the rehearsal period, in a bid to create a sense of familiarity between Fox, Eccleston and McGregor which befitted their characters. McGregor believed that this technique really paid dividends once filming began.

'The most important thing about the film is the [characters'] relationship in the flat and the fact that they've lived together far too long,' he explained. 'And that rehearsal period was brilliant from the word go. We used to get up, have breakfast and do scenes in our pyjamas. In a rehearsal room, you'd set up chairs and tables, and pretend there was a wall there

In preparation for his role as Dean Raymond in the offbeat surfing drama *Blue Juice*, McGregor took surfing lessons with his co-stars Sean Pertwee, Steven Mackintosh and Peter Gunn

adopting different dialects for his film and TV work, and initially felt uncomfortable using his own speaking voice.

'It's weird to be doing something in my own accent because it makes me feel very naked,' he laughed. 'It's also the first thing that I've done in contemporary clothes, which is much harder because I've got nothing to hide behind – no cravats, no English accent.'

Shallow Grave entered production in the last week of September 1993. While exterior photography took place in such locations as the Royal Alexandria Hospital, Edinburgh's New Town, the forest of Rouken Glen, Paisley Mortuary and the newrooms of Glasgow's *Evening Times*, the majority of shooting occurred in a converted warehouse on a Glaswegian industrial estate, which doubled as Juliet, David and Alex's flat. At 90 x 150 ft, the makeshift soundstage comprised a bathroom, kitchen, lounge and hall as well as four bedrooms, and thus

formed Scotland's biggest-ever indoor set.

Due to the film's tight budget and breakneck schedule, the cast and crew had to work hard to get *Shallow Grave* in the can. 12-hour working days were common, as the production seemed to lurch from one crisis to another. At one point, Macdonald and crew even looked set to run out of 35mm film, until the financiers finally agreed to intervene!

Yet in spite of it all *Shallow Grave* was completed on schedule, and its making would be remembered fondly by its cast and crew. McGregor particularly enjoyed working with the film's leading triumvirate, Danny Boyle, Andrew Macdonald and John Hodge and savoured the spirit of team work which they cultivated on the set. He was also delighted that they gave his mother, Carol, a small cameo role in the film, as one of the potential flatmates to whom Juliet, David and Alex give the cold shoulder.

Once filming was completed, the cast and crew went their separate ways, leaving Boyle, Macdonald and Hodge to complete the picture. The end product would surpass even the most optimistic expectations of its makers. Shocking, thrilling and utterly absorbing, *Shallow Grave* is a bold and dynamic movie which boasts three compelling performances from Fox, Eccleston and McGregor.

The film's qualities weren't missed by critics or cinemagoers, who made *Shallow Grave* one of the most successful productions of 1995. Critics showered the production with rave reviews, while the movie grossed more than £20 million in box office receipts, making it one of the most profitable releases of the year. As if that wasn't enough, it went on to receive several accolades, including BAFTA's prestigious Alexander Korda Award for the most outstanding British film of the year.

Besides Boyle, Macdonald and Hodge, the biggest benefactor from *Shallow Grave*'s huge popularity was Ewan McGregor, whose dark and edgy performance as Alex Law was widely considered as one of the film's main treasures. Within weeks of the film's launch, he was being hailed as 'The Next Big Thing' and one of Britain's brightest hopes. It was a label he would more than live up to with his second collaboration with the famed Boyle-Macdonald-Hodge dream team, *Trainspotting*.

Before that fateful reunion, however, McGregor kept himself busy with a further string of film and TV appearances. After completing his work on *Shallow Grave*, the young actor returned to England to shoot a guest-starring role in an episode of *Kavanagh, QC*, a new legal drama series devised as a vehicle for former *Sweeney* and *Inspector Morse* star John Thaw. In *Nothing But the Truth*, McGregor plays David Armstrong, a university student who stands accused of rape. Kavanagh befriends the young man and manages to win his acquittal, only to be faced with evidence suggesting his client's guilt during a shocking denouement.

Although Ewan gave a solid performance as the not-so-innocent defendant, his work on *Kavanagh, QC* would do nothing for his career

other than provide another credit on his resumé and some spare cash. Ironically, though, his appearance on the show was destined to have a huge impact on his life. While filming *Kavanagh*, McGregor met Eve Mavrakis, a French production designer four years his senior. Ewan and Eve (pronounced 'Ev') immediately hit it off and swiftly embarked on a whirlwind romance which would culminate in their marriage less than two years later.

Following *Kavanagh*, McGregor remained on the small screen for his next outing, in the one-off BBC comedy-drama *Doggin' Around*. The production toplined film veteran Elliott Gould (*M*A*S*H*, *Nashville*) in a rare television role as Joe Warren, an American jazz pianist who is forced to make a living by touring various clubs in Northern England. While McGregor clearly enjoys himself as a member of Warren's band, *Doggin' Around* was largely overlooked by viewers and remains one of his least-seen offerings.

McGregor fared little better with his following project, *Blue Juice*. A low-budget British movie funded by Channel 4. Carl Prechezer's offbeat drama stars Sean Pertwee (*Event Horizon*, *I. D.*) as J. C., a 29-year-old surf champion who is forced to choose between a life on the ocean's waves and his commitment to his long-suffering girlfriend, Chloe (*The Mask of Zorro*'s Catherine Zeta Jones). J. C.'s struggle to reach a decision is further complicated by the arrival of some old friends from London, including Dean Raymond (McGregor), a psychotic drugs dealer.

Blue Juice was shot on location in Cornwall, south-west England, during the cold winter months of October and November 1994. In preparation for his role, McGregor joined his fellow castmembers Sean Pertwee, Steven Mackintosh and Peter Gunn for surfing lessons before the start of filming. The quartet soon became good friends and began to socialise with each other off-set.

'I had a great time filming in Cornwall for ten weeks,' McGregor later recalled in

Although the film was poorly received by most viewers, McGregor clearly had a great time during the making of *Blue Juice*. 'I've never partied so much in my life,' he subsequently explained

Undoubtedly the actor's most unusual and most explicit project to date, *The Pillow Book* featured McGregor in a series of nude scenes

Details magazine. 'I've never partied so much in my life.'

Unfortunately, while its cast and crew had a terrific time , the film itself proved to be a far less enjoyable experience for most viewers. Despite Pertwee's best efforts, J. C.'s central dilemma never really rings true, leaving viewers indifferent about his character's fate. As for McGregor, he succeeds in capturing Dean Raymond's irritating qualities a bit too well, and delivers one of the few truly annoying performances of his career.

McGregor himself would often try and defend the film, but even he knew he was fighting a losing battle. 'It's a good laugh,' he insisted in *Details*, before admitting the film's shortcomings. 'I mean, it's a bit muddled in the middle ... It's just a shame, it's not really very good.'

As soon as *Blue Juice* had wrapped, McGregor began work on his most bizarre project to date, *The Pillow Book*. Billed as a tale of love, obsession and fetishism, *The Pillow Book* was written and directed by cult

body as the paper. The couple's bliss soon turns to despair, though, when Nagiko begins to write on other men's bodies. In a desperate bid to win back her affections, Jerome tries to fake his suicide – and accidentally manages to kill himself! The climax of the film reveals how Jerome's exhumed body becomes the eponymous 'Pillow Book' of skin and poetry.

Shot on location in Luxembourg, Hong Kong and Japan, *The Pillow Book* was filmed between the end of 1994 and beginning of 1995, with a budget of £2 million. McGregor felt drawn to the project by the idea of working with Greenaway and was particularly intrigued by his unusual script, which placed an emphasis on stunning visual detail rather than dialogue.

'This was a very different experience for me, but I found it very stimulating,'. 'I regularly spent between two and four hours having calligraphy applied all over my body – very sensual and something I will not forget in a long while!'

Besides meeting the demands of the calligrapher, the film also required McGregor to spend a great deal of his time in front of the cameras naked. Once again, the actor threw himself into the part and gave a no-holds-barred performance which would be remembered by many of his female fans as his finest hour!

However, in the months leading up to the film's release, McGregor became increasingly concerned about how his parents would react to the most explicit performance of his career. Fortunately, Carol and James both felt that the film was 'beautiful' and didn't seem too uncomfortable with its love scenes. In fact, James even joked that he was pleased to see that his youngest son had inherited one of his finest assets!

Carol and James McGregor's response to *The Pillow Book* proved to be unusual, though. A true love-it-or-loathe-it experience, the film was embraced by the art-house crowd, but was simply too obtuse for a mass audience. Nevertheless, the film did offer further proof of Ewan McGregor's versatility and his willingness to take risks. And it was those two qualities which led to his major breakthrough in *Trainspotting*.

McGregor spent between two and four hours a day having calligraphy applied all over his body to play Jerome, an English translator who becomes the eponymous Pillow Book of skin and poetry!

film-maker Peter Greenaway, whose credits include such equally unique outings as *The Draughtsman's Contract* and *The Cook, The Thief, His Wife and Her Lover*.

The film stars *The Last Emperor*'s Vivian Wu as Nagiko, a young woman desperate to find her Mr Right: namely, a man who is as good a lover as he is a calligrapher. After a long search, Nagiko finds happiness with Jerome (McGregor), an English translator who convinces her to actually take up calligraphy herself and allows her to use his

TICKET TO RIDE

4

As the star of *Trainspotting*, McGregor offered a compelling portrait of youth which proved to be his ticket to the Big Time

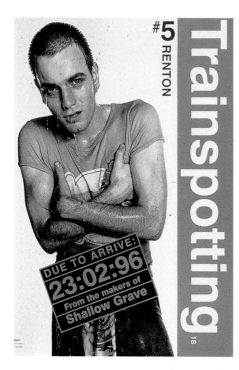

The image of McGregor as the alienated drug addict Mark Renton in *Trainspotting* was embraced by the fashion industry, and swiftly established the Scottish actor as a cultural icon across the globe

The surprise success of *Shallow Grave* turned its creative masterminds into the talk of Hollywood. Within weeks of the film's release, director Danny Boyle, producer Andrew Macdonald and writer John Hodge were being courted by some of the film industry's leading movers-and-shakers. Boyle was invited to helm projects involving the likes of Sharon Stone and Gene Hackman, while the entire triumvirate were offered $250,000 by producer Scott Rudin (*The Firm*, *Sabrina*) to collaborate with him on their next project. Ultimately, though, the group would ignore the call of Hollywood and remain in Britain for their next project, *Trainspotting*. And they would call upon their 'Fourth Musketeer', Ewan McGregor, to topline a film that was destined to become an international smash hit and cultural phenomenon.

Even before their first outing had been released, the *Shallow Grave* to decided that they would continue to work together as a team. It was Andrew Macdonald who first suggested that their second project should be an adaptation of Irvine Welsh's cult novel. Macdonald had read the book shortly after *Shallow Grave* completed filming and was simply stunned by Welsh's powerful, insightful and occasionally surreal portrait of drug addiction, with its incredible highs and its terrifying lows. Convinced that it could make an equally outstanding movie, Macdonald took the idea to his colleagues.

Their reaction was mixed. While Boyle immediately loved the idea, Hodge was not

convinced that it could be done. The writer pointed out that Welsh's book was little more than a series of brilliant vignettes and lacked a central narrative drive, and was also concerned that a film adaptation could be too bleak for most viewers. Nevertheless, Hodge did agree to give the project a go and joined his colleagues on a trip to the Scottish cities of Edinburgh and Glasgow, where they spent time with real-life heroin users in an attempt to learn as much as the could about drug culture.

Renton discovers that his psychotic friend, Begbie (Robert Carlyle), isn't amused by jokes about his sexuality in a typically hilarious yet shocking scene from *Trainspotting*!

As with his previous film, *Shallow Grave*, director Danny Boyle assembled the cast of *Trainspotting* – including Ewen Bremner, Ewan McGregor and Robert Carlyle – for two weeks of rehearsals prior to the start of filming, to enable them to establish a chemistry and sense of rapport between one another

Hodge had completed his first 40-page draft of *Trainspotting*'s screenplay by November 1994. The script used one of the book's characters, Mark Renton, as its protagonist, and took him through a series of events and monologues from Welsh's novel, as he battles to overcome his heroin addiction and 'Choose Life' – a normal, drug-free existence. As the script was further adjusted and rewritten, Renton increasingly emerged as an anti-hero for modern times.

Normally, finding funding for a project so potentially controversial as *Trainspotting* would be tricky, but thanks to the success of *Shallow Grave*, Boyle, Macdonald and Hodge managed to secure £1.5 million from Channel 4 in March 1995. Ironically, though, one problem that did have to be resolved before the start of filming was the ownership of rights to Welsh's novel, which belonged to

another production company. After much wrangling, the firm sold Channel 4 the rights for a reported £30,000 and a share of the film's profits.

Once *Trainspotting* entered pre-production, its makers turned their attention to the matter of the film's casting. In keeping with their love of team work, Boyle, Macdonald and Hodge were keen to employ as many members of *Shallow Grave*'s cast as they could and roles were found for both Keith Allen and Peter Mullan in the new film. Newcomers to the 'family' included Ewen Bremner (*Naked*, *Judge Dredd*) as the dim-witted no-hoper Spud, Jonny Lee Miller (*Hackers*) as the selfish Sick Boy, Kevin McKidd (*Small Faces*) as the ill-fated Tommy and Robert Carlyle, who in a slight twist of fate beat *Shallow Grave*'s Christopher Eccleston to the role of Begbie, a psychopathic criminal with a penchant for gratuitous violence. Completing the line-up of Renton's so-called friends, screen newcomer Kelly Macdonald was picked out of hundreds of girls to play his under-age girlfriend, Diane, after responding to a series of adverts placed by Boyle which asked, 'Are you the new Kate Moss or Patricia Arquette?'

As for the crucial role of Renton himself, that would go to an actor without any audition or interview. From an early point in the production, *Trainspotting*'s leading role was earmarked for McGregor, whom Boyle in particular thought was simply perfect for the part. The actor was first shown the film's script while promoting *Shallow Grave* at the Sundance Film Festival in the USA.

'It was the kind of part you don't read very often,' he explained, 'and it was exactly the part that I personally felt I wanted to play at the time. I was looking for the part of Mark Renton and there it was – even better than I could have hoped for, because John Hodge is such a brilliant writer.'

Despite McGregor's enthusiasm for his script, Hodge initially had his doubts that McGregor was suitable for the role and had to be convinced that the rising star was the right choice by Boyle and Macdonald. Fortunately, he soon realised that he couldn't have dreamed of finding a better Renton.

McGregor's preparations for the role were thorough and uncompromising. Besides having a razor-sharp crew cut, the actor lost two stones in weight by adhering to a strict diet, which consisted of special meals and required him to give up beer, milk and butter. His hard work swiftly paid off: within six weeks, he had begun to look ill enough to pass as a drug addict.

The actor also heavily researched the subject of drug abuse and read everything he could about heroin. Towards the end of filming *The Pillow Book*, he even began to hang around train stations in Luxembourg to study the behaviour of junkies, one of whom inspired Renton's stooped posture. McGregor had to rely on observation and research, because the former Crieff native had very little

first-hand knowledge of drug abuse that he could draw on.

'We didn't really do any drugs because there weren't any to be had,' he told *Paper Magazine*. 'I missed the whole rave scene and the 'E' culture in the late 1980s. It's quite sad. They really got the wrong guy for the job: Ewan 'Mr Nae Drugs' McGregor.'

One thing McGregor didn't do in preparation for the project, though, was sample heroin. From the very beginning of his career, he had never subscribed to the process of 'Method Acting', and could happily drop in and out of character at a moment's notice. And the more he learned about heroin and drug abuse, the more he was determined never to fall foul of the problem.

'Any mystique I had before about heroin is completely gone now,' McGregor revealed in *Paper Magazine*. 'I'm not as judgmental about drug addicts as I used to be. I know more about their suffering, their pain and their need for help.'

A weak and frail-looking McGregor joined the cast of *Trainspotting* in Glasgow at the beginning of May 1995, for two weeks of rehearsals. Besides running through scenes together, the group met with recovered addicts from the Calton Athletic drugs rehabilitation unit to discuss their experiences and learn how to accurately fake drug-taking. The actors also attempted to develop an easy rapport and a sense of camaraderie which befitted their characters, and watched a number of films together which Boyle hoped that *Trainspotting* would emulate in terms of style, such as *Goodfellas*, *Near Dark*, *The Hustler* and *A Clockwork Orange*.

Once the rehearsal period was over, *Trainspotting*'s seven-week shoot began on 22nd May. Filming predominantly took place in Glasgow, which doubled as Edinburgh, and with the production based at the converted Wills Cigarette Factory.

Like *Shallow Grave* before it, *Trainspotting* was an ambitious project produced on a relatively low budget. Once again, resources were tight and the schedule gruelling. The making of the film was particularly hard on

Above: McGregor lost two stones in weight to play *Trainspotting*'s Mark Renton

Middle: Renton offers Spud (Ewen Bremner) helpful advice on how to make the wrong impression during a job interview!

Top: Temporarily free of their drug addiction, Renton and Sick Boy (Jonny Lee Miller) look for other 'hobbies' to occupy their time

Above: The *Trainspotting* cast were thrashed by members of the Calton Athletic drugs rehabilitation unit during a football match

Middle: Trainspotting was the toast of numerous film festivals, including Cannes

Top: Prior to *Trainspotting*, Ewan 'Mr Nae Drugs' McGregor had absolutely no experience or knowledge of drug-taking or heroin abuse

McGregor, who not only had to capture the complexity of Renton's character, but was also required to work for 34 of the production's 35 shooting days. Unsurprisingly, it was a physically and mentally-draining process. Take, for example, the filming of the scene in which Renton is hit by a car as he flees from the police after a shoplifting spree. This five-second sequence took over two hours to perfect, during which time McGregor was 'run over' around 20 times!

Another memorable scene involves Renton's visit to the 'Worst Toilet in Scotland', where his search for a pair of opium suppositories takes him round the bend – literally. According to McGregor, that shocking sequence was as difficult to film as it is to watch.

'Oh God, yes, all the toilet stuff was very bleak,' he later recalled in *Empire*. 'It's true to say that I felt a bit sick that day. That day was like, "Please can I get off this set, it's disgusting." It was horrible.'

Yet in spite of such horrific moments, McGregor had one of the most exciting and rewarding experiences of his entire career on *Trainspotting*. He enjoyed being reunited with Boyle, Hodge and Macdonald, and once again savoured the enthusiastic and creative atmosphere they established on set.

With filming completed by mid-July, *Trainspotting* began eight weeks of post-production before its first private screening in November. The film was subsequently launched in February 1996, when it was rightly heralded as an instant classic.

By turns hilarious, harrowing, insightful, wonderful and shocking, *Trainspotting* is a truly awe-inspiring film. Danny Boyle's remarkable direction combines gritty realism with moments of surreal brilliance, while John Hodge's fast-paced script moves from one classic sequence to another, offering an entertaining but cautionary tale of drug abuse and all its trappings. The film's cast are uniformly excellent, with special kudos going to Robert Carlyle's terrifying yet amusing portrayal of the foul-mouthed Begbie and McGregor's mesmerising central performance as Mark Renton.

Predictably, however, upon its release *Trainspotting* was swiftly accused of glamourising heroin-taking. And as the film's star, Ewan McGregor faced most of these accusations himself. In a series of interviews, the actor firmly dismissed such claims, on the grounds that *Trainspotting* showed all the dangers and evils of drug addiction.

'I don't think this film will promote heroin use at all,' he stated in *The List*, 'unless people are stupid.'

Ultimately, though, the controversy surrounding *Trainspotting* only served to give the film added publicity and helped make it one of the most financially-successful projects of the decade. Besides being a smash hit in Britain, the film was also hugely popular in America – albeit thanks to a re-dubbed soundtrack, in which the actors attempted to play down their Scottish dialects. *Trainspotting* went on to gross a staggering $70 million, making it the year's most profitable film in the world, and the second most successful British movie of all time, pipped only by the feel-good romantic comedy *Four Weddings and a Funeral*.

In wake of their film's success, Danny Boyle, Andrew Macdonald and John Hodge once again found themselves being touted as the saviours of British cinema. With

The production of *Trainspotting* was very hard on McGregor, who worked 34 of the production's 35 shooting days. Fortunately, he loved every minute of it – apart from the scene in which Renton takes a dive down the 'worst toilet in Scotland'!

Trainspotting, it seemed the triumvirate had fulfilled the promise of *Shallow Grave* to produce one of the finest British films of all time, and had thus taken their place among the world's most exciting film-makers.

Trainspotting had an even stronger effect on its leading man. Within weeks of the film's release, Ewan McGregor was well on his way to becoming a household name on both sides of the Atlantic. And as critics praised his bold and compelling portrayal of Renton, McGregor was showered with such accolades as a nomination for Best Breakthrough Performance at MTV's Movie Awards and *Empire*'s Best Actor of the Year.

McGregor also found himself embraced by popular culture as an icon for today's alienated youth, while the image of Renton inspired fashion commentators to refer to skinny models as being part of the 'post-*Trainspotting* wave.' The actor's place at the cutting-edge of pop culture was confirmed by his frequent appearances on the covers of style magazines, as well as his subsequent selection to become one of the first male models to feature in the famed Pirelli Tire Calendar, in 1997.

Whereas many people would have problems dealing with such a powerful wave of instant popularity, McGregor took everything in his stride and refused to become a victim of his own hype. For example, when asked how he felt about being described as 'the best actor of his generation', McGregor jokingly demanded that his interviewer should simply refer to him the as the best actor *in the world*! Similarly, despite his place at the cutting-edge of fashion, he maintained that he had little interest in the subject and found it all rather pointless.

As the *Trainspotting* phenomenon exploded, McGregor was actually getting used to his new life as a husband and a father. Immediately after the film finished production, he had decided to tie the knot with his girlfriend, Eve Mavrakis.

The wedding took place in France in July 1995, and held an almost surreal quality for McGregor. Fresh from the set of *Trainspotting*, the groom didn't exactly look his best, as he was still underweight and sporting Renton's short crew-cut hairstyle. Even more bizarrely, the ceremony was conducted in French, which meant that he didn't understand a word of it and pledged his undying love by saying 'Oui' at the moment he guessed was right!

Ewan became a father for the first time the following February, when Eve gave birth to their daughter, Clara Mathilde McGregor. Upon returning home after the happy event, the 24-year-old actor telephoned all of his relatives and friends to share the good news. In his enthusiasm to make his calls, however, McGregor hadn't realised that it was the middle of the night!

The young actor swiftly adjusted to his new responsibilities of life as a husband and father, complete with its daily 6:30am start and such challenges as babysitting and nappy-changing. He also had to find a bigger home for his family, which culminated in their relocation to the trendy St. John's Wood area of London in 1997. Despite his new commitments, though, McGregor refused to give up his regular drinking sessions with pals, and maintained his passion for fast motorbikes.

While promoting *Trainspotting* at the Cannes Film Festival shortly after Clara's birth, McGregor was surprised by most people's response to the news that he was a married man with a child. But he was even more stunned when a style magazine labelled his wife and daughter as 'fashion accessories'!

'People are incredibly rude about it sometimes,' the actor noted in *Elle*. 'Like, "What? You're married?" Strange reaction to have. Proves what people's ideas about marriage are. "We're having a baby." "What?" As if it's the end of the world. Of course, it's the start of a brilliant world.'

Ewan McGregor's world was looking equally brilliant on a professional level. But now the test would be whether or not he could consolidate the phenomenal success of *Trainspotting*, rather than just slowly fade away into obscurity.

Opposite: **Immediately after he finished working on *Trainspotting*, McGregor headed for France, where he married his girlfriend, Eve Mavrakis. The couple had a daughter, Clara Mathilde, the following year**

Above: **Despite his new commitments as a husband and father, McGregor remains a passionate drinker and motorcyclist!**

SCOTTISH EXPORT

5

Following the success of *Trainspotting*, McGregor was determined not to sell-out to the Hollywood dream

In McGregor's mind, the feel-good costume drama *Emma* was the perfect antidote to the agony and the ectasy of *Trainspotting*

By the time the *Trainspotting* phenomenon exploded at the beginning of 1996, Ewan McGregor had already finished working on two further films: the lavish period piece, *Emma* and the contemporary British drama, *Brassed Off*. Both would provide a vivid contrast to his portrayal of Mark Renton and also demonstrated the Scottish actor's determination to avoid being typecast at all costs.

Emma was McGregor's first taste of big-budget, American-style movie-making. For although the film was shot in Britain and based on the popular Jane Austen novel, it was funded by major American studio, Miramax, produced and directed by American artists, and toplined an American actress, Gwyneth Paltrow (*Seven*, *Sliding Doors*) as the eponymous Emma Woodhouse. McGregor knew that it wasn't going to be any ordinary production from his very first day on the set, when he was assigned the biggest trailer of his career to date.

The movie follows Miss Woodhouse's attempts to play matchmaker for those around her and boasts an unusually strong supporting cast, which includes Toni Collette (*Muriel's Wedding*), Greta Scacchi (*Presumed Innocent*, *Heat and Dust*), Jeremy Northam (*The Net*, *Mimic*) Alan Cumming (*GoldenEye*), Juliet Stevenson (*Truly Madly Deeply*) and of

course, Ewan McGregor, who makes a brief appearance as the caddish Frank Churchill. Frank initially seems to be a contender for Emma's hand in marriage, but really has no interest in the young Miss Woodhouse as he is secretly engaged to another.

'Frank Churchill is the life and soul of the party,' McGregor said of his character. 'Sickeningly so. It's all, "Ha, ha, ha, Frank's here, now the fun will start." But there's a reason for this over-the-top heartiness. He's secretly engaged to Jane and knows the rich aunt who had adopted him in London will not approve the match. So when he makes one of

his periodic visits to Highbury to see his father, he makes a big thing of playing the field by flirting with everything in skirts!'

McGregor agreed to star in the feel-good costume drama primarily because he felt that it would make a refreshing change from *Trainspotting*. He certainly wasn't attracted to the project by Jane Austen's novel, which he publicly referred to as being 'terribly tedious' and at one point even described it as 'a good book to take to bed because it sends you to sleep.'

Unfortunately, he would later come to doubt the wisdom of his decision to appear in

the film, as *Emma* proved to be one of the biggest disappointments of his career. Although the film is a fine, if unremarkable, adaptation of Austen's novel, McGregor delivers a painfully limp and unconvincing performance as Frank Churchill. The actor himself was not blind to his failure and would later claim that he spent so much time perfecting Frank's classical English accent that he forgot to decide upon the correct manner in which he should play the character.

'I think the film's all right but I was so crap, I was terrible in it,' McGregor admitted with typical candour in *Time Out*. 'I didn't believe a

Emma **featured one of the weakest performances of McGregor's career, and the actor himself was the first to admit it. 'I was so terrible in it,' he explained. 'I didn't believe a word I said.'**

Brassed Off was a terrific showcase for McGregor. Besides appearing in several powerful scenes and embarking on an onscreen love affair with Tara Fitzgerald, the actor also seized the chance to demonstrate his expertise with the French Horn

word I said. I just thought, 'Shut the f*** up, Frank.' It was the first time for me. I was really embarrassed about it.'

Moving on from *Emma*, McGregor promised himself that he would do better in his next project, *Brassed Off*. And he certainly kept his word, as the film marked a welcome return to form for the Scottish star.

Written and directed by Mark Herman, *Brassed Off* offers a touching portrait of life in a Yorkshire mining community. As the local colliery's brass band prepares for a national music competition, its members are forced to confront the closure of their mine. The ever-reliable Pete Postlethwaite (*In the Name of the Father*, *The Lost World: Jurassic Park 2* and *The Usual Suspects*) toplines the film as Danny, a terminally-ill conductor who struggles to keep the band together as their lives fall apart, while McGregor co-stars as Andy, a young musician who becomes romantically involved with a colleague, Gloria (*Sirens* star Tara Fitzgerald), only to learn that she has a secret agenda.

Besides the opportunity to work with Herman and Postlethwaite, McGregor felt attracted to *Brassed Off* by its powerful portrayal of a community on the edge of destruction. He also liked the idea of playing a nice and straightforward character, to whom he could relate much more easily than most of his screen counterparts. The actor joined the production in its second week of filming, immediately after completing his work on *Emma*.

Brassed Off was destined to be an outstanding blend of drama, comedy and pathos, which provided McGregor with another chance to shine. The role of Andy allowed him to run the full gamut of emotions between joy and despair and also presented its own particular challenges. Not only did the young Scotsman have to employ a believable Yorkshire accent, but he also had to play the French Horn. In both regards, McGregor succeeded admirably, and was especially pleased to display the musical skills he had acquired at Morrison's Academy as a child.

Despite his fast-growing popularity among movie-makers, though, McGregor was never one to subscribe to the traditional divide between film and TV, which dictates that actors cannot shift between the two mediums. Consequently, he agreed to guest-star in an episode of the long-running American horror anthology series, *Tales from the Crypt*, when the production relocated to London towards the end of 1995. In *Cold War*, McGregor plays an ordinary American whose girlfriend has an affair with another man, only to learn that her new lover is a vampire! The episode required its leading guest artist to employ an American accent and also featured *Absolutely Fabulous* star Jane Horrocks, with whom McGregor would later appear opposite on the big screen in *Little Voice*.

During the early part of 1996, McGregor decided that the time had come to head for Hollywood. His choice seemed to bow to convention and follow the classic examples of actors like Gary Oldman, Ralph Fiennes and Daniel Day Lewis, who had used their success in Britain as passports to a series of roles Stateside. However, McGregor insisted that he was merely trying his hand at a new form of film-making adamant that he had no intention of basing his career in the States.

'I've always wanted to go to Hollywood and drive big cars and be in big movies,' he said at the time. 'But I don't f***ing want to get caught in that thing we saw in [the British documentary series] *Hollywood Men*, where they'll do anything to become a star.'

Thanks to *Trainspotting*, McGregor had received a wealth of scripts and lucrative offers from Hollywood producers, most of whom saw the young star as the natural successor to his fellow Scotsman, Sean Connery. After discussing all his options with his wife Eve, McGregor eventually chose *Nightwatch*, a $10 million thriller produced by Dimension Films, a division of Miramax. McGregor had struck a good working relationship with the company during the production of *Emma*, and liked the sound of *Nightwatch*, which was a remake of the acclaimed Danish thriller *Nattevagten*, and was set to be helmed by the original film's director, Ole Bornedal. Upon signing a contract, the actor started packing his bags and polishing his American accent.

Nightwatch stars McGregor as Martin Belos, a law student who takes a part-time job as a security guard in a morgue to help pay his bills. However, shortly after he accepts the post, a serial killer begins to stalk the city. Assigned to find the murderer, Inspector Cray (Nick Nolte of *48 Hrs* and *Prince of Tides* fame) finds a series of clues which all point to Martin's guilt.

For McGregor, *Nightwatch* offered a fascinating taste of the Hollywood dream. While he enjoyed his time on the film and particularly liked working with Nolte, he was less impressed by what he learned about big-budget movie-making.

From the beginning, McGregor was aware of the emphasis on commerce over art and realised that his casting had nothing to do with talent, but simply reflected his 'marketability' as the star of *Trainspotting* and *Shallow Grave*. But as the weeks went by, he felt increasingly frustrated with the impersonal, businesslike approach which characterised both the set and, it seemed, most of Hollywood's movers-and-shakers.

'When I met with agents in L.A., they would tell me you had to do two movies for yourself and then two for the business,' McGregor revealed in *Entertainment Weekly*. 'And I thought, "F*** off. No, you don't. You do every film because you want to do good work; because you're interested in making good movies and working with good people." To do a crappy event movie for a lot of money, like *Independence Day* – I would never taint my soul with that crap.'

The actor also tired of living in Los Angeles and started to crave for the countryside. To soothe himself, he watched golf on television and would recall how he used to play the sport when he was growing up, until he decided to 'retire' due to the fact that he wasn't very good.

On the plus side, McGregor did enjoy the perks of celebrity, such as his big trailer on the set of *Nightwatch* and the chauffeur-driven limos to and from the stage. His highlight of the entire experience, though, was seeing the film's trailer for the first time, when he heard his name delivered in that classic American trailer-speak.

'I've realised I've been waiting my whole life for that guy to say my name,' McGregor

Scream on: After much consideration, McGregor chose to make his Hollywood debut with the Miramax shocker *Nightwatch*

Although he tried to make the most of his time in Hollywood, McGregor's experiences during the making of _Nightwatch_ confirmed many of his fears about big-budget movie-making

laughed in _Elle_. 'He just drives from one nightclub to the next in a big old car, eating glass and smoking Marlboros and drinking scotch! And then he goes, "Ewan McGregor!"'

Despite the trailer's best efforts, _Nightwatch_ was destined to be a critical and commercial disappointment. Several months after principal photography had concluded, a number of its castmembers, including McGregor, were called back to re-shoot certain sequences which apparently had

failed to generate the required response in test screenings. Then, when the film was finally released in April 1998 (almost two years after its production), _Nightwatch_ proved to be little more than an upmarket slasher flick, packed with gore but largely devoid of any real sense of mystery or suspense. Despite a sterling central performance from McGregor, the film was slated by reviewers and generally avoided by cinemagoers.

True to his word, as soon as he had finished his work on *Nightwatch*, McGregor headed for Ireland's County Clare to star in a European production, *Serpent's Kiss*. The actor had first expressed an interest in the project during the autumn of 1995, after he had read Tim Rose-Price's screenplay. On hearing of McGregor's interest, the film's producer, Robert Jones, deliberately delayed its start date by nine months, to allow the actor to fit it into his hectic schedule. Although he had received a number of more lucrative offers by the time *Serpent's Kiss* entered production and was not legally bound to the project, McGregor maintained his original commitment and reported to the film's set in time for the beginning of shooting in summer 1996.

Set in Gloucestershire in 1699, *Serpent's Kiss* stars McGregor as Meneer Chrome, a Dutch landscape gardener who becomes caught in a web of sexual intrigue revolving around the wife of one his employers, Julianna Smithers (Greta Scacchi). McGregor's co-stars include *Brassed Off*'s Pete Postlethwaite and *Withnail & I*'s Richard E. Grant.

For McGregor, the filming of *Serpent's Kiss* was something of a busman's holiday. The shooting schedule was very relaxed and gave him plenty of free time to spend with his wife and daughter in Ireland, where he was delighted to explore the countryside following his stay in Los Angeles.

Upon returning to his London home in September, McGregor felt refreshed and ready for even more work. After recording an advert for Virgin Atlantic Airlines, he headed to Bournemouth to shoot a short film, *Swimming with the Fishes*. The project was directed by Justin Chadwick, with whom the actor had previously collaborated on *Family Style* in 1993, and McGregor agreed to appear primarily as a favour to his old friend. Billed as a tale of sexual intrigue set in a fish and chip shop, *Swimming with the Fishes* took a mere five days to film.

Flitting from the glorious excesses of Hollywood to the lowest end of independent film-making, it was plain for all to see that Ewan McGregor was no ordinary star. And while his next project would take him back to the States, it would not be any ordinary American blockbuster.

After the glorious excesses of *Nightwatch*, McGregor headed for Ireland to star in the medium-budget period drama *Serpent's Kiss*

Once the *Nightwatch* experience was behind him, McGregor seemed even more resolute that he would never base his career in Hollywood.

'I don't like it there,' he told *Empire* magazine in a recent interview. 'The way they just talk business; it has got nothing to do with making good films. The studio system in L.A. is about A-list, B-list, C-list. About money. They just make me cold and they turn out such awful crap.'

OUT OF THIS WORLD

6

Marking McGregor's third collaboration with the *Trainspotting* team, *A Life Less Ordinary* was never going to be a conventional production

As the end of September 1996 drew near, Ewan McGregor eagerly prepared to join forces with director Danny Boyle, producer Andrew Macdonald and writer John Hodge for a third time. Hot on the heels of *Shallow Grave* and *Trainspotting*, the creative triumvirate had called upon the actor to star in their latest effort, a whimsical romantic comedy entitled *A Life Less Ordinary*.

John Hodge first began developing *A Life Less* Ordinary directly after he had written *Shallow Grave* in 1993, but the project had been put on the backburner when he and his colleagues turned their attention to *Trainspotting*. Following the latter's release, Hodge returned to his earlier script, then entitled *A Life Less Unusual*. After 18 rewrites, what started out as a road movie set in France and Paris became the tale of a Scottish drifter in America, who kidnaps his boss's daughter after he loses his job as a janitor and finds love courtesy of unearthly forces.

As Hodge readied his screenplay for production, Danny Boyle and Andrew Macdonald were considering a lucrative offer from the Fox Film mega-corporation to direct

Above: Desperate to regain his job as a janitor, Robert (McGregor) takes his boss' daughter, Celine (Cameron Diaz) hostage in *A Life Less Ordinary*

Opposite: An improvised bank heist ends in disaster for Robert

Out of this World

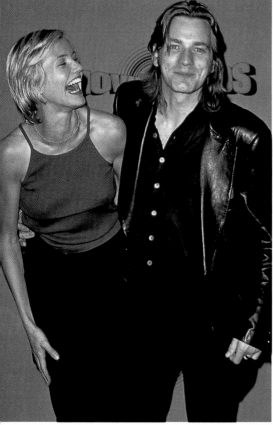

McGregor and Diaz worked hard at developing a believable chemistry for their characters, and became firm friends behind the cameras

and produce *Alien Resurrection*, the fourth film from the celebrated science fiction film franchise. Although both liked the movie's script and were excited by the prospect of working on such an epic production, ultimately they decided to stick to their roots and continue their collaboration with Hodge.

After securing *A Life Less Ordinary*'s $12 million budget from a consortium of companies, the team turned their attention to casting. From the outset, Hodge had written the film's leading role with Ewan McGregor in mind, and he was always the team's first choice for the role of Robert. However, the actor was committed to working on *Serpent's Kiss* at the time of the production's original start date in June 1996, forcing Boyle and company to look elsewhere.

Following a series of meetings with the likes of Hollywood superstar Brad Pitt, the team decided that they just couldn't make the film without McGregor and changed its production schedule to accommodate him. Having agreed to change Robert's nationality from Scottish to American, Boyle and company then toyed with the idea of asking McGregor to use his American accent from *Nightwatch*, but ultimately returned to their original concept for the movie.

McGregor was delighted to join forces with the Boyle-Macdonald-Hodge dream team yet again, for whom he claimed he would do just about anything. On reading the script for their latest venture, he was especially excited by the opportunity of starring in the type of old-fashioned romantic comedy that he had always adored since childhood.

'I really look forward to reading everything John [Hodge] has written because it's always so unexpected and so funny,' the actor said upon joining the project. '*A Life Less Ordinary* was everything I could have hoped for and I jumped at the opportunity to do it.'

With McGregor in place, the team then chose the film's leading lady. After interviewing five famous American actresses, the role of Robert's hostage/love interest, Celine, went to rising star Cameron Diaz (*The Mask*, *My Best Friend's Wedding*). The rest of the cast swiftly fell into place, with Academy Award-winning actress Holly Hunter (*The Piano*, *Always*) and Delroy Lindo (*Crooklyn*) coming aboard to play the pair of angels who

are assigned to play reluctant matchmakers for Robert and Celine, while Ian Holm (*The Fifth Element*, *Brazil*) agreed to portray Celine's villainous father, Mr Naville.

As with the director's two previous films, Boyle decided to assemble *A Life Less Ordinary*'s principal cast together a couple of weeks before shooting, to allow them to rehearse and establish a sense of mutual understanding. Besides running through scenes and discussing certain aspects of the film, McGregor, Diaz, Hunter and Lindo participated in such activities as visiting a shooting range, where they practised handling and using firearms. The group also watched two classic movies which Boyle felt reflected the style of his latest venture, namely the Clark Gable-Claudette Colbert romantic-comedy *It Happened One Night* and *A Matter of Life and Death*, which shows how Heaven can interfere with earthly events.

Boyle was particularly keen for McGregor and Diaz to develop a special chemistry, which he felt would be central to the film's success. One night, he even went as far as to take the two stars to a 'red-neck' Karaoke bar in America's deep south, where they were forced to jump on stage and sing together in a moment highly reminiscent of a scene in the film! Much to their director's delight, the pair hit it off from their very first meeting, and fast became friends.

'I loved working with Cameron,' McGregor later said of his co-star. 'She's brilliant fun on and off the set, and I think that comes across in her performance.'

Diaz was equally complimentary about her leading man. 'All the girls have been coming up to him and saying, "Ewan McGregor, we're in love with you. You're married and have a baby – it's not fair,"' the actress revealed in *Details* magazine. 'He has a fun, sophomoric sense of humour – we joke on the set about having gas! And he makes acting seem so easy: he doesn't beat himself up over it.'

A Life Less Ordinary's 50-day shoot began on 30 September 1996, and took place in a variety of locations in and around Salt Lake City, Utah. While McGregor would slowly get used to his character's distinctive hairstyle, which he christened the 'Bullethead' look, he never felt comfortable staying in such a

conservative area as Utah. He soon grew tired of being questioned about his age every single time he visited a store to buy some cigarettes and was particularly taken aback to people's response to his rather unusual headwear.

'I've got a black woollen hat and it's got 'Pervert' written across the front of it,' he explained in *Elle*. 'It's the name of a clothing label. And I was with my wife and my baby at the supermarket and I didn't think. I just put my hat on Clara's head, because it was cold. And the looks [I got]! I couldn't figure out why I was getting death looks. And then I realised my 10-month-old baby's wearing a hat with the word 'Pervert' written on it, and these people were like, "There's Satan! There's Satan out with his kid!"'

'And then,' McGregor added with a wide grin, 'I made a point of wearing it every time we went out!'

Despite his reservations about staying in Utah, McGregor thoroughly enjoyed his actual working experience. As always, he expressed his joy at working with Boyle, Macdonald and Hodge, and once again felt that they succeeded in establishing a creative but relaxed atmosphere on set. The actor particularly appreciated the way their latest collaboration offered a subversive take on the romantic-comedy genre, and relished the opportunity to demonstrate his flair for comedy.

'I do tend to be cast as cynical characters, but *A Life Less Ordinary* is a love story – albeit of an odd sort – and I play a sweet, innocent guy,' McGregor noted in *Film Review*. 'Everything's going a bit weird for him though, and there's more humour in this than anything I've previously done.'

The movie also contains McGregor's tribute to one of his favourite rock bands, Oasis. McGregor frequently socialised with the British group's members and delivers his own unique version of one of their tracks, *Round Our Way*, in the scene where Robert

While he loved the idea of playing an innocent character in a whimsical romantic comedy, McGregor was less enamoured by Robert's 'bullethead' hairstyle

Above: McGregor goes Wild in the outrageous Glam Rock drama *Velvet Goldmine*

Top: The third season *ER* episode *The Long Way Round* earned McGregor a prestigious Emmy Award nomination

returns to his cabin with groceries for the recently-kidnapped Celine.

Filming of *A Life Less Ordinary* wrapped in December 1996 and the finished product was launched across the world the following autumn. Inevitably, the movie was almost universally regarded to be a disappointing follow-up to the glorious highs of *Shallow Grave* and *Trainspotting*. While Boyle's celebrated visual flair is well in evidence and the cast acquit themselves well, *A Life Less Ordinary* is an awkward blend of comedy, romance and fantasy which fails to engage the audience's interest or emotions in quite the way it should. As a result, the film went to become one of the biggest flops of 1997, grossing less than $10 million in America and Britain.

Fortunately, the movie's failure did little to tarnish McGregor's reputation. His portrayal of Robert was one of *A Life Less Ordinary*'s few strengths, and by the time it reached the big screen, the busy actor had already made two further films.

Upon wrapping *A Life Less Ordinary*, McGregor remained in the States to shoot an episode of America's top-rated drama series, *ER*. He had landed a guest-starring role in the show after a series of talks with NBC TV executives, who wanted to capitalise on his popularity from *Trainspotting*. While the Studio attempted to sell the idea to McGregor on the grounds that it would bolster interest in his upcoming movie and would also increase his own public profile, the main reason why he agreed to guest-star on *ER* was simply because he considered himself a fan of the show.

The actor's appearance came in the third season episode, *The Long Way Around*. It was a highly unusual instalment of *ER* because it largely takes place outside Chicago Cook County Hospital and primarily focuses on two characters: series regular Nurse Carol Hathaway (Julianna Margulies); and a Scottish petty criminal, Duncan Stewart (McGregor). When Duncan's attempt to rob a convenience store goes horribly wrong, he decides to hold the customers

as hostages, including Nurse Hathaway. Hathaway and Duncan slowly build a rapport, but he is subsequently shot by a policeman and dies in the Emergency Room.

McGregor savoured his week on the show and was particularly pleased to meet the regular cast of *ER*, whose on-screen exploits he had been following for the past two years. His appearance in the series was aired on 13 February 1997 and was nominated for a prestigious Emmy Award for Outstanding Guest Performance on a Drama Series.

Returning to England at the end of 1996, McGregor settled down to what he hoped would be his first holiday in two years. For once, he had resisted the temptation of a string of projects, and promised himself a well-earned rest. Unfortunately, though, it wasn't meant to be. Shortly into his holiday, the actor's daughter, Clara, fell ill with a suspected bout of meningitis. Although she eventually recovered and regained her full health, Clara's sickness ensured that McGregor's vacation was infinitely more stressful than the making of any film he could have appeared in.

Once Clara had recovered, McGregor began to attend meetings with prospective employers and prepared to start work on his next project, *Velvet Goldmine*. Written and directed by cult film-maker Todd Haynes (*Safe*, *Poison*), the movie offers a gritty portrait of Britain's Glam Rock scene during the 1970s. *Michael Collins* star Jonathan Rhys-Meyers toplines as Brian Slade, a rock megastar who fakes his own death to escape the music business. When a British journalist (*Empire of the Sun*'s Christian Bale) attempts to investigate Slade's mysterious disappearance 10 years later, he learns about the bisexual rocker's wild antics, including his infatuation with American rocker Curt Wild (McGregor).

For McGregor, starring in *Velvet Goldmine* represented a chance to take his childhood dream of becoming a rock star to the most extreme level possible. To play the appropriately-named Curt Wild, McGregor

studied videos of Iggy Pop (upon whom his character's outrageous dance moves were loosely based), and was also coached by the film's executive producer, REM star Michael Stipe, about the art of live performance. The actor used his newly-acquired skills in a scene which required him to sing in front of more than 200 extras. In true McGregor-style, the sequence ends with his character baring-all to the crowd!

Velvet Goldmine was another unusual and daring choice on McGregor's part. Few established leading men would accept a supporting role in a project destined for cult status, let alone agree to shoot a gay love scene. McGregor, however, was intrigued by the film's premise and vowed to give the most outrageous performance of his career, the 'highlights' of which would include a homosexual love scene with co-star Christian Bale shot on a London rooftop.

Ewan McGregor's shocking exploits in *Velvet Goldmine* couldn't be any further removed from his next project, which would blast him into deep space and make him a noble hero for children across the galaxy.

With roles in projects as diverse as *A Life Less Ordinary* and *Velvet Goldmine*, McGregor consolidated his reputation as one of the most unpredictable and versatile actors working today

STAR WARRIOR

7

By landing the role of young Obi-Wan Kenobi in the eagerly-awaited new *Star Wars* films, McGregor is set for global superstardom

After a series of meetings and auditions, McGregor was overjoyed to learn that he had won the coveted role of Obi-Wan Kenobi in the *Star Wars* prequels

On his first day of shooting *Velvet Goldmine*, Ewan McGregor received the phone call he had been dreaming of for nearly 20 years. Following a series of interviews, auditions and screen tests, the 26-year-old Scottish actor learned that he had won a leading role in the long-awaited new *Star Wars* films.

McGregor's casting ended a guessing game which had started two years earlier, when *Star Wars* creator George Lucas first announced his intention to re-launch the legendary science fiction film franchise. During a rare interview with leading industry newspaper *Variety* in May 1995, Lucas confirmed that he was in the process of planning three prequels which would take place before the events depicted in the original *Star Wars* trilogy. The self-made movie mogul went on to reveal that besides writing and financing the prequels, he would also helm the first instalment of the new trilogy himself, thus making it his first directorial outing since the original *Star Wars* way back in 1977.

While Lucas was understandably tight-lipped about the storylines of the new films, he did reveal that they would chart the rise and fall of Anakin Skywalker (Luke and Leia's father) and explain how the greatest Jedi Knight in the galaxy was seduced by the dark side of the Force to become the evil Darth

As the young Obi-Wan Kenobi, McGregor follows in the footsteps of Sir Alec Guinness, who played the noble Jedi Knight in the original *Star Wars* trilogy

Vader. Consequently, the films would predominantly feature new characters, with only Anakin Skywalker/Darth Vader, the revered Jedi Knight Obi-Wan Kenobi, the Jedi Master Yoda and the loveable droids R2-D2 and C-3PO playing significant roles in both trilogies.

As soon as news of Lucas's return to the *Star Wars* saga became public, rumours began circulating about who would star in the prequels. Mark Hamill, alias Luke Skywalker in the original trilogy, emerged as a clear favourite to play Anakin, while esteemed British actor Kenneth Branagh was widely

reported to follow in the footsteps of Sir Alec Guinness by playing Obi-Wan Kenobi. A more bizarre rumour suggested that Obi-Wan would actually be portrayed by an unknown actor with a computer-generated image of a 20-year-old Alec Guinness superimposed over his face!

The long process of casting the first instalment didn't begin in earnest until 1996, though, when Robin Gurland began to interview prospective candidates. Gurland had the pick of the world's leading actors and actresses for the roles, with virtually everyone clamouring for a place on the call sheet of one of the most eagerly-awaited films of the century. It would take her a year to finalise her choices, with the official announcement coming in June 1997.

One of the most difficult roles to cast was that of the young Obi-Wan Kenobi. For Gurland, the challenge was to find a young leading man who could not only combine an inner strength with a sense of recklessness, but could also stand up to comparison with the great Alec Guinness. To make matters worse, Obi-Wan was one of the few characters set to appear in all three films, meaning that there was simply no margin for error.

Among the first actors to meet with Gurland was Ewan McGregor, who originally discussed the project with her at the beginning of 1996, just as *Trainspotting* threw the actor under the spotlight. A year later, McGregor was invited to see Gurland again and further meetings with George Lucas and producer Rick McCallum followed. The actor's final hurdle came in March 1997, when he filmed a screen-test with his future co-star, Liam Neeson, to see if they had the required mentor-student chemistry. Evidently they did, as both actors went on to star in the film.

McGregor reportedly fought off strong competition from the likes of Brad Pitt, Leonardo DiCaprio and, of course, Kenneth Branagh to win the role of Obi-Wan Kenobi and was told the good news on the first day of filming *Velvet Goldmine*. However, as Lucasfilm wished to keep the prequel's casting a secret until the official announcement later in the year, the actor was sworn to secrecy about the nature of his next assignment. McGregor duly obliged, sharing this exciting development with only his wife and parents, and leaving the cast and crew of *Velvet Goldmine* to decide for themselves why he seemed so deliriously happy at the start of filming.

Winning a role in the new *Star Wars* films was like a dream come true for McGregor. Not only had the original movies captured his imagination as a child and inspired him to become an actor, but he also had a personal link with the saga thanks to his uncle, Denis Lawson (alias the X-Wing pilot Wedge Antilles in the original trilogy). Consequently, McGregor had given little thought to accepting the part of Obi-Wan Kenobi; he always instinctively wanted to be a part of the movies.

'When you're my age, and you were out there cheering when the first *Star Wars* came out, what are you going to do when they offer you one of the leads in the new film? Say, "No, no way!,"' he laughed in *Total Film*.

McGregor joined a highly-impressive list of actors cast in the new *Star Wars* film. Top of the Call Sheet was Liam Neeson, the Academy Award-nominated star of *Schindler's List*, *Michael Collins* and *Rob Roy*, who landed the movie's leading role as a character described only as a 'venerable Jedi Knight' (but rumoured to be named Qui-Gon Jinn). Nine-year-old child actor Jake Lloyd (*Jingle all the Way*) was cast in the pivotal part of the nine-year-old Anakin Skywalker, and 16-year-old Natalie Portman (*Leon*, *Mars Attacks!*) beat the likes of *Titantic*'s Kate Winslett to the role of 'The Young Queen' (reportedly called Padme) destined to become Anakin's wife, and the mother of Luke and Leia Skywalker.

The film's supporting artists included *Star Wars* alumni Kenny Baker, Frank Oz and Ian McDiarmid, all of whom were asked to reprise their roles as R2-D2, Yoda and the scheming Senator Palpatine from the original trilogy. Anthony Daniels also won a return invitation to the saga to voice an early version of his famous counterpart, C-3PO, while Warwick Davis (the Ewok Wicket in *Return of the Jedi*) shot a brief scene as a Tatooine trader. Among the newcomers to the saga were such familiar actors as Terence Stamp (*Priscilla: Queen of the Desert*, *Superman 2*), Brian Blessed (*Flash Gordon*), Adrian Dunbar (*Hear My Song*) and

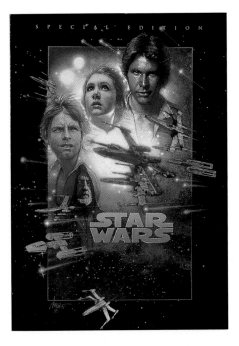

From his very first meeting with the film's casting director, McGregor was sworn to secrecy about his involvement with the *Star Wars* saga. In the absense of any firm details about the new film, fans began to dissect every single detail about the production – including reports which claimed that McGregor had braids weaved into his hair to play young Obi-Wan Kenobi

After attending the British premiere of the revamped *Star Wars: The Special Edition* in March 1997, rumours began to circulate suggesting that McGregor would be involved in the prequels. Such reports were not officially confirmed until three months later

Pulp Fiction star Samuel L. Jackson, who famously secured a cameo role as a Jedi Knight after a phone call to George Lucas.

By agreeing to appear in the *Star Wars* prequels, McGregor had become a part of one of Hollywood's most lucrative film franchises. Although the first instalment's budget was initially estimated at a conservative $40 million, the film would ultimately cost around three times that amount to produce, due largely to the demands of its ground-breaking special effects. It would also be one of the most heavily-merchandised projects in movie history: besides the inevitable action figures, books, comics, computer games and T-shirts, the prequel was also part of a $2 billion sponsorship deal between Lucasfilm and the Pepsi Corporation. Yet McGregor firmly maintained that he hadn't broken his stand against blockbuster movie-making by joining the *Star Wars* franchise, and dismissed claims that he was 'selling out' his artistic integrity.

'These movies are very different,' he insisted in *Total Film*. 'The great thing is that I can do these films and not have to bother doing a blockbuster again. I can just get on with the kind of movies that I want to do.'

One of the many unique aspects surrounding the production of a *Star Wars* film is its commitment to complete and utter secrecy. George Lucas's determination to keep the prequel's plot under wraps before its release would reach almost absurd heights during the film's production. From the moment he first met with Robin Gurland to discuss the role, McGregor was sworn to secrecy about the project. When he landed a role in the movie, he joined the rest of the film's cast and crew by signing a non-disclosure clause in his contract, which banned him from discussing any of the film's story details. The production itself was filmed behind closed doors, to ensure that details of Neeson, McGregor and Lloyd's epic struggle against the evil Sith Warriors remained out of the public domain.

Lucas wasn't content at keeping the movie's storyline a secret, though. In a bid to preserve an air of mystique around the production, the writer-director refused to reveal the names of new characters, only referring to them by vague descriptions. Similarly, he would not even be drawn on the film's title. As rumours began to circulate suggesting that the movie would be called *Balance of the Force*, *Knights of the Force*, *Genesis*, *The Beginning* or *Guardians of the Force*, Lucas would only refer to the project by its shooting title, *Star Wars: Episode One*.

Another way in which Lucas attempted to keep fans and reporters off the trail was by deliberately delaying the announcement that *Episode One* had began filming. While press releases claimed that the movie would enter

production in September, shooting actually commenced on 3rd June.

Filming began in Tunisia, Morocco, which doubles as Anakin Skywalker's homeworld, the desert planet of Tatooine. Three weeks later, the cast and crew headed for Leavesden Studios, London, where the majority of shooting would take place. After a brief excursion to the Caserta Royal Palace in Italy (which serves as the 'Young Queen's Palace') at the end of July, shooting returned to Leavesden, where principal photography was completed on 26 September 1998. A series of reshoots would take place the following year, in the run-up to the film's eagerly-awaited release in the summer of 1999.

In McGregor's mind, the biggest challenge of playing Obi-Wan Kenobi, revered Jedi Knight and master of the Force, was to successfully capture Alec Guinness's famed dialect. To this end, he studied many of the legendary actor's films, including the original *Star Wars*.

'I have to get his accent,' McGregor explained to *Entertainment Weekly*. 'He's got this very specific older man's voice. It'd be great if I could trace it back to his youth and get it right.'

From an acting standpoint, *Star Wars: Episode One* proved to be something of an unsatisfying experience for McGregor. While he had loved working on performance-based

For McGregor, the biggest challenge of playing Obi-Wan Kenobi was capturing Alec Guinness' distinctive accent and giving it a youthful spin

Above: McGregor's co-stars in the Star Wars prequels include such familiar characters as C-3PO, R2-D2, Yoda and Jabba the Hutt, as well a host of new computer-generated aliens and robots

Opposite: Although McGregor left the set of *Episode One* feeling unfulfilled from an acting standpoint, he never had any doubt that the finished film would be 'magic'

projects like *Trainspotting* and *Shallow Grave*, most of his work on *Episode One* required him to act opposite thin air, which was destined to be filled by an unprecedented number of state-of-the-art special effects. He also felt restricted by the film's often-elementary dialogue. Ultimately, however, the sheer joy of being involved with the *Star Wars* saga was more than enough to keep him on cloud nine.

'They're hard work those movies,' McGregor told *The Big Breakfast*. 'You don't sit and bang out the scenes and then work with scenes and get into the actor thing that we like to do, because there are so many other things going on around you or things that will be there behind you or whatever. So it's a slog, really. But every day I had a *Star Wars* moment where I would go, "Ahh ... I'm in *Star Wars*!"'

One of McGregor's most cherished *Star Wars* moments came when he donned Obi-Wan Kenobi's outfit for the first time and christened himself 'Jedi McGregor'. Another

was the opportunity to use a lightsabre – yet much to his embarrassment, his first bout of interstellar swordplay was destined to be left on the cutting room floor.

'The first take and my lightsabre literally flew out of my hands,' the actor admitted in *Cinescape*. 'No one tells you the sabres have about 10 'D' batteries in them. They numb your hands. I tossed the sabre up in the air and it ended up hitting a technician in the head!'

Much to the comfort of his colleagues, McGregor soon mastered the use of his lightsabre and apparently made quite an impressive swordsman – although the actor himself would later claim that neither he nor Liam Neeson could compete with their child co-star, 'lethal' Jake Lloyd.

As well as building a strong working relationship with his cast and crewmates, McGregor also enjoyed spending time with his director, George Lucas. The actor was impressed by the movie mogul's visionary mind and his down-to-Earth attitude, while Lucas was delighted with Ewan's work, publicly describing him as both a worthy successor to Alec Guinness and the new Harrison Ford. Lucas also joined McGregor and his uncle, Denis Lawson, for lunch one day when Lawson visited the set. However, like many actors before him, McGregor did admit to being occasionally thrown by the movie mogul's famed minimalist direction.

'It was overwhelming the first time he said, "Okay, you come in the spaceship, you start it up..."', McGregor laughed in *Film Review*. 'And we were suddenly on the floor laughing. You come in the spaceship and start it up. I wonder how that is? Is there a key?'

According to McGregor, moments like that demonstrated that *Episode One*'s emphasis was on adventure and special effects rather than acting. This was further illustrated by the fact that the film required some 18 months of pre-production and a further 18 months of post-production, but only three months of filming. Shortly after he had finished his work as Obi-Wan Kenobi, he realised that his thoughts echoed those of his illustrious predecessor.

'I looked at an interview Alec Guinness did when he played Obi-Wan,' McGregor revealed in *Cinescape*. 'He said, "My feeling about *Star Wars* is that I delivered the lines and I hope they do the backgrounds nicely." I feel the same way.'

Despite his minor frustrations working on the film, McGregor still cherished every single moment of his time on *Star Wars: Episode One*. He felt honoured to be a part of the project and savoured all of its unique pleasures, from acting opposite R2-D2 and Yoda to flying through space and using a lightsabre. He was also thrilled by the prospect of being immortalised as a young Obi-Wan Kenobi action figure, which he looked forward to giving to his young daughter. Above all, though, he always remained absolutely convinced that the finished product would be an astonishing piece of film-making which would delight cinemagoers of all ages around the world.

'Can you imagine what it'll be like sitting down in some screening room, the curtain goes up and there it is – the new movie?' the actor enthusiastically predicted in *Total Film*. 'Magic.'

ROGUE SUPERSTAR

8

Blissfully unaffected by success, Ewan McGregor refuses to bow to convention and continues to pursue his career on his own terms

After battling the forces of evil in the sci-fi blockbuster *Star Wars: Episode One*, McGregor returned to Earth to appear in the low budget drama *Little Voice*

As the world held its breath for the return of *Star Wars*, it was business as usual for Ewan McGregor. While he had thoroughly enjoyed his first excursion to a galaxy far, far away, the actor remained passionately committed to his crusade to play diverse roles in a wide range of projects. He certainly had no intention of resting on his laurels in the wake of his *Star Wars* experience; nor would he let the legendary science fiction franchise completely overhaul the course of his career.

'In my life, it was another job,' he explained in *Film Review*. 'Of course, it is a huge job because it's *Star Wars*. But I've got a body of work behind me. I don't feel like, "Oh I've made it." I feel like, "Oh, I'm in *Star Wars*."'

True to form, by the time principal photography on *Star Wars: Episode One* had concluded, Britain's busiest young star had a string of projects lined up. And they were all light years away from the adventures of Obi-Wan Kenobi and his fellow masters of the Force.

Immediately after *Episode One*'s wrap party, McGregor headed for Scarbrough, north-east England, to begin work on *Little Voice*. An adaptation of Jim Cartwright's play *The Rise and Fall of Little Voice*, the low-budget character piece was directed by Mark Herman, with whom the actor had previously worked on the acclaimed *Brassed Off*. McGregor's willingness to appear had actually helped Herman secure funding for the

project, and the director returned the favour by basing the production's schedule entirely around its leading man, to ensure that he could complete his work on the film as quickly as possible.

Little Voice stars Jane Horrocks as a shy woman who dreams of becoming a singer. With the help of her friend, Billy (McGregor), she manages to overcome her shyness and reveals her inestimable talent to an unsuspecting public. But her career hits a sour note when she falls foul of a crafty music agent, Ray Say (Michael Caine). For

McGregor the film represented a welcome return to performance-based film-making after the special effects extravaganza that was *Star Wars*, and offered him the opportunity to work with screen icon, Michael Caine. In another change from the *Star Wars* saga, the film also allowed McGregor to bare all for the cameras yet again.

During the filming of *Little Voice*, the Ewan McGregor phenomenon took a further step forward, as the actor scored his first hit record in the British charts. PF Project's *Choose Life* featured McGregor's now-legendary 'Choose Life' monologue from *Trainspotting* and immediately raced to the top of the pops. The track's success came as a huge surprise to its lead vocalist, as McGregor didn't even know of its existence until he heard the record while relaxing at a Scarbrough disco!

McGregor completed his work on *Little Voice* on Friday, 17 November 1997 and reported to the set of his next film the following day. Based on a true story, *Rogue Trader* toplines the Scottish star as Nick Leeson, the high-flying derivatives broker responsible for the collapse of the Barings

Never one to play it safe, McGregor stars as the disgraced derivatives broker Nick Leeson in the controversial bio-flick *Rogue Trader*

Little Voice allowed McGregor to make his welcome return to performance-based movie-making

Bank and who was ultimately convicted for fraud.

From its development, *Rogue Trader* was always destined to be a controversial project. As an adaptation of Leeson's official biography, the film suggests that he was framed for the Barings Bank's demise and depicts him as an innocent victim of a conspiracy. The movie gained further notoriety when tabloid reports claimed that Leeson was set to make a healthy profit from the film.

As the controversy raged, McGregor took a diplomatic line. In a series of interviews, he maintained that he had no personal views on Leeson's guilt or innocence and was happy to leave cinemagoers to make up their own minds about him.

However, the actor was far less happy when the tabloid press erroneously claimed that he was having an affair with his co-star, Anna Friel (*Brookside*), who had been cast as Leeson's wife. McGregor had long feared becoming the target of such coverage and furiously dismissed such claims.

While *Rogue Trader* was still being shot, McGregor joined forces with his actor-friends Jude Law (*Gattaca*), Sadie Frost (*Shopping*), Jonny Lee Miller (*Trainspotting*'s Sick Boy) and Sean Pertwee (*Blue Juice*), as well as

producers Damon Bryant and Bradley Adams, to set up the British production company, Natural Nylon.

Inspired by the example of America's United Artists studio, Natural Nylon was established with the goal of producing high quality, low-to-medium budget films, in the hope of stopping British talent fleeing to America in pursuit of work. The first word of the company's title illustrated its commitment to natural, artistically-driven projects, while Nylon was an anachronym for its bases in New York and London. Natural Nylon's seven founders each took equal shares in the firm and agreed to devote some of their time to the company's productions, while maintaining a degree of freedom to pursue their own separate projects.

Away from the set of *Rogue Trader* and the offices of Natural Nylon, McGregor realised that he could no longer keep up with his rapidly-increasingly fan mail and decided to hire an assistant. His mother, Carol, promptly gave up her teaching job to act as the star's personal assistant.

With *Rogue Trader* completed by the end of January, McGregor took a month off before travelling to Tunisia to participate in the first of a series of re-shoots for *Star Wars: Episode One*. He then headed for Montréal, Canada, to star in an independent movie, *Eye of the Beholder*. Directed by Stephan Elliott (*The Adventures of Priscilla: Queen of the Desert*), the $15 million thriller is an adaptation of Marc Behm's novel and toplines McGregor as a private detective who becomes obsessed with a mysterious woman, only to discover that she is a serial killer. McGregor's co-stars included *A Time to Kill*'s Ashley Judd, *Beverly Hills 90210* heart-throb Jason Priestley, singer K.D. Lang and *Sleeping with the Enemy*'s Patrick Bergin.

Shortly afterwards, McGregor was linked to an American art house flick, *South from Hell's Kitchen*. An intimate character study, the film was set to star Bridget Fonda (*Jackie Brown*, *Scandal*), Jean Rochefort and McGregor as a prostitute, mental patient and drifter respectively and explores how each find new meaning in their lives during their stay in a mental institution.

Upon returning to the U. K., McGregor headed for Ireland, to star in his first Natural

Nylon production, *Nora*. Based upon the life story of Nora Barnacle, the film features Susan Lynch (*The Secret of Roan Inish*) in the title role and McGregor as her screen husband, the famous poet James Joyce. The film would also mark McGregor's first foray into the producer's chair.

Nora was McGregor's seventh film project in less than two years. Once again, it seemed that the actor's passion for his work was getting the better of him. Even he was at a loss to explain why he was so busy.

'I've always been fiercely driven and I'm still driven now,' he mused in *Film Review*. 'Maybe now more than ever, because I can't stop it. They keep giving me scripts, I keep f***ing doing them. I can't say no.'

Just when it looked like the actor was about to take a break, news emerged that he had started rehearsing for his first stage production in five years. Based at the Hampstead Theatre Club, *Little Malcolm and his Struggle Against the Eunochs* was set to star McGregor as the leader of a group of rebellious art students who take a stand against censorship. Not only did the 1960s' farce provide McGregor with yet another chance to rebel against the system, but it also marked his long-awaited first collaboration with his uncle, Denis Lawson, who directed the play.

Beyond that, McGregor had a packed schedule in place which would take him well into the next millennium. His first port of call was *Don't Think Twice*, a film comedy about a struggling rock 'n' roll band which again was set to be directed by his Uncle Denis. The actor was then linked to an adaptation of Iain Banks's psychological thriller *Complicity*, an epic prison drama in which he would co-star with George Clooney and a film biography about Beetle icon John Lennon. Ironically, by the time he had learned about the latter production, reports had already began to circulate claiming that Lennon's widow, Yoko Ono, had given her blessing to McGregor's casting!

In addition to his own projects, McGregor also had to deal with his commitment to Natural Nylon. The actor was lined-up to star in two of the company's productions: a film biography of politician John Wilkes, and *The Hellfire Club*, a $8 million period piece which would feature all five of Natural Nylon's actor-founders.

McGregor's more ambitious future plans include starring in his first French-language film. Since the birth of his daughter, Clara, in February 1996, the actor has been learning French, fuelled by the fear that if he didn't master the language, his bilingual child could one day ridicule him in French without him knowing! The actor has also heard that the French find it sexy to hear their language spoken with a Scottish accent and wants to put this theory to the test.

Despite his incredible drive and enthusiasm, there simply aren't enough hours in the day for McGregor to do every project that catches his interest. One of his biggest disappointments was that he was unable to appear in *Alien Love Triangle*, the fourth film made by the *Shallow Grave*, *Trainspotting* and *A Life Less Ordinary* triumvirate. McGregor was further upset by reports claiming that the lead role in their fifth outing, *The Beach*, was set to go to *Titantic* sensation, Leonardo DiCaprio, whom the film's financiers felt had more box office clout than the Scottish star.

From a purely commercial point of view, McGregor's replacement by DiCaprio seemed justifiable. Prior to *Star Wars: Episode One*, McGregor had deliberately avoided appearing in anything vaguely resembling a potential blockbuster and the remarkable financial success of *Trainspotting* and *Shallow Grave* couldn't compare with the takings of *Titanic* or *Independence Day*. Hence, in *The Hollywood Reporter*'s 1998 round-up of the world's most bankable stars, the Scottish star was ranked a respectable but hardly Earth-shattering 56th, while in *Film Review*'s survey of the 50 hottest young talents in the world, he came seventh, behind the likes of Tom Cruise, Will Smith, Matt Damon and DiCaprio.

All that will change, however, in the wake of *Star Wars: Episode One*. Although the box office failures of productions like *Godzilla*, *Speed 2* and *The Postman* have shown that no film is a sure thing, the new *Star Wars* looks virtually certain to redefine box office records and should topple *Titanic* as the most successful film of all time. In the process, Ewan McGregor seems destined to be blasted into interstellar superstardom – a

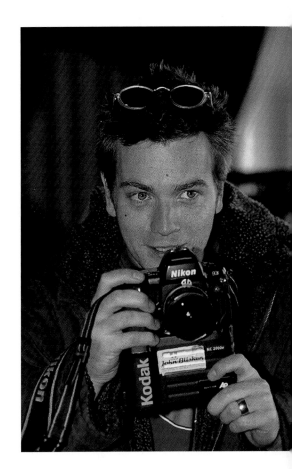

During the filming of *Little Voice*, McGregor learned that he had produced his first hit record with PF Project's *Choose Life*

Rogue Superstar

McGregor will have plenty of opportunities to shine in the second and third *Star Wars* prequels, which promise to reveal how his character is partly to blame for the downfall of the Old Republic and the creation of Darth Vader

fabled place where no-one will ever doubt his box office credentials again.

Of course, the big worry is that just about everything else in McGregor's life and career will change after *Episode One*'s debut on 25 May 1999. The original *Star Wars* forever typecast two of its three leads, namely Mark 'Luke Skywalker' Hamill and Carrie 'Princess Leia' Fisher, and it took Harrison Ford several years and a series of outstanding films to escape the shadow of Han Solo. A number of the trilogy's supporting castmembers also found work impossible to come by once the galactic rollercoaster ride was over and were forced to make a living by touring the Star Wars convention circuit *ad infinituum*.

McGregor, however, is optimistic that his career won't fall foul of the so-called '*Star Wars* curse.' The actor points to the fact that he already had a body of work behind him before he joined the saga and feels pretty secure in the knowledge that he shouldn't be typecast as Obi-Wan Kenobi.

That isn't to say, though, that McGregor intends to leave the character behind following the release of *Episode One*. On the contrary, he is committed to playing Obi-Wan Kenobi in a further two *Star Wars* prequels, which are set for release in 2001 and 2003. And whereas the actor had felt slightly unsatisfied by the first outing's emphasis on action and adventure over characterisation, the second and third instalments promise to satisfy his deepest desire for drama, tragedy and pathos, by depicting Anakin Skywalker's descent into darkness. As Obi-Wan Kenobi, McGregor will not only have to face being betrayed by his former friend and pupil, but will also bare some of the blame for Anakin's fate, as well as the annihilation of the Jedi Knights and the downfall of the Galactic Republic – which should be more than enough for the actor to sink his teeth into!

While Ewan McGregor clearly has a great deal ahead of him, there can be little doubt that he is already guaranteed a place in the annuls of film history. In the space of a decade, the former high-school drop-out and RADA-reject has become an international superstar and icon, who is applauded by critics and cinemagoers alike. And few actors can compete with the speed and ease of his meteoric rise to the top of his profession.

'I didn't ever have to do those struggling years,' he once reflected in *Empire*. 'I'm not guilty about it anyway, a lot of actors want you to feel guilty about that. I didn't get the job to be unemployed and I've learnt a lot from every job I've done since. I'm aware of where I am and how tasty my path here has been.'

McGregor, perhaps surprisingly, has remained exceptionally unaffected by stardom, his central goal for the future is

simply to continue acting for a living. Although he has moved into producing as a result of his involvement with Natural Nylon, acting is his driving passion, and he has little interest in writing, directing or just about any other profession. In fact, McGregor simply can't foresee the day when he decides to stop acting, or imagine that anything could ever beat the thrill of seeing one's own work on the big screen.

'I love watching myself up on screen,' he told *Ministry*. 'It's f***ing great. I love it because I'm so proud to be up there. I still can't believe I'm up there.'

You'd better start believing it, Ewan. Because as we enter the third millennium, few people in the world will doubt that Ewan McGregor has made it to the big screen super league. The Force, it seems, has been with him all along.

21st century boy: Ewan McGregor has risen to the top of his profession with an ease most actors can only dream of. And the future has never looked brighter

SELECTED CREDITS

FILMS

1993 **Being Human**

1994 **Shallow Grave**

1995 **Blue Juice**

1995 **The Pillow Book**

1996 **Trainspotting**

1996 **Emma**

1996 **Brassed Off**

1997 **A Life Less Ordinary**

1998 **Nightwatch**

1998 **Velvet Goldmine**

1998 **The Serpent's Kiss**

1998 **Little Voice**

1998 **Rogue Trader**

1998 **Eye Of The Beholder**

1998 **Nora**

1999 **Star Wars: Episode I**

TV

1992 **Lipstick on Your Collar**

1993 **Scarlet & Black**

1994 **Kavanagh, QC (Guest star: Nothing But the Truth)**

1994 **Doggin' Around**

1996 **Tales From The Crypt (Guest star: Cold War)**

1996 **Karaoke**

1997 **ER (Guest star: The Long Way Around)**

9